COMMON SENSE TAROT
The Complete Guide to Tarot Reading

by Camden Benares

Edited by Ed Buryn and Robin Quinn
Copy edited by Gina Renée Gross
Designed by Michele Lanci-Altomare & Bertram Gader

A NEWCASTLE BOOK
First Printing September 1992
10 9 8 7 6 5 4 3 2 1
Printed in the United States of America

CONTENTS

INTRODUCTION
by Mary K. Greer

"The purpose of reading a book is to inform and entertain," said Mortimer Adler and Charles Van Doren in their invaluable classic, *How to Read a Book*. We can say the same of reading the Tarot, for as Camden Benares claims, the Tarot cards are for storytelling. "I use them to tell a story that relates to your life in some way," he explains. The information on which this story is based comes from the meaning of the individual cards and the significance of their positions in the layout. Knowledge of human behavior and insight from the client's presentation of self, verbal and nonverbal, will also add to the reading.

This book is written for the individual who would like to tell entertaining stories for friends and clients, giving information about people's lives based on the book's direct and straightforward interpretations of the cards. Given some time and effort, according to Benares, these basic meanings can be memorized. The book also provides a variety of layouts that emphasize different kinds of information that go into making up the story one tells. In keeping with his intention of entertainment, the author's interpretations are simple and affirmative. He likes to encourage the client to discern his or her own potential for achievement. How useful this story actually is, Benares emphasizes, should be left totally up to the client. All decisions resulting from the reading are made only by the client who is responsible for determining his or her own future.

To entertain with Tarot implies that the client will be amused or diverted in the process of having his or her cards read. According to the American Heritage Dictionary, such entertainment involves "formal, deliberate acts of bringing about pleasure." Thus, Tarot reading can be a deliberately agreeable way to occupy both oneself as reader and another person as client. I can personally vouch for the pleasure that Tarot brings, for I have been entertained by the cards for nearly a quarter of a century. I can foresee the pleasure they give continuing for at least as long into the future.

Entertainment is also about holding one's attention, about contemplation, and maintaining a thought in one's mind. A Tarot reading, giving as it does a reflection in symbols of a situation in one's life, helps the person to focus on that situation. But, rather than maintaining old patterns and thinking in ruts, previously unseen dynamics of the situation and their ripple effects often appear. Therefore, a reading gives the client the opportunity to widen his or her perspective. The reading encompasses, as a layout usually does, the past, present, and future as well as the possible effects of a variety of factors on the client's life. What could be more fascinating to anyone than a picture of his or her life and its possibilities?

In *How to Read a Book*, Adler and Van Doren do add one more purpose to those traditionally given for reading a book, which is to increase our understanding through our own efforts. As they express it, "With nothing but the power of your own mind, you operate on the symbols before you in such a way that you gradually lift yourself from a state of understanding less to one of understanding more. Such elevation . . . is highly skilled reading."

An alert and honest reader, as they point out, feels sometimes the "shock of puzzlement and perplexity." By developing his or her skills in understanding, the reader can meet this challenge. When you, as either the reader or the client, increase your understanding by discovery of the source of what puzzled you in either your own life or in the story as told in a reading, you rise in your own estimation. You find that you can defer to your own authority. You can begin to consider yourself—and your own mind—as a respected repository of great wisdom.

Camden Benares says that Tarot can increase our self-esteem and enjoyment in life. We increase our pride and self-respect when we make changes in our own lives by honoring greater possibilities than those we previously accepted. As Benares discovered through Tarot read for him, "Being shown a wider point of view opened me up to new ideas and greater possibilities that in turn led to significant changes in my life."

To be informed is to know simply that something is the case. To be entertained is to know pleasure in the experience. To be enlightened is to know, in addition, what is meant and why it is so. If a reading has given the client information that seems valid, that client must then ask about its significance in his or her life. While this is the client's responsibility and therefore beyond the scope of this book, I would like to encourage the potential reader of the Tarot to offer this possibility to the client by asking how the information relates to his or her life and what the client has learned from the reading. The client, of course, has no obligation to answer. But both reader and client can have the opportunity to discover a greater truth through this synthesizing process than was apparent from the information alone. Thus by entertaining the reading in the mind and hospitably welcoming personal assertions, information can lead to the pride and respect of self-discovery.

May you find in this book an entertaining and commonsense introduction to the art of reading the Tarot.

1

About Tarot Reading

Perhaps the greatest benefit of becoming a Tarot-card reader is the increase that you will experience in knowledge and intuitive ability. Every reading adds to the Tarot reader's knowledge of human beings and of the world in ways that few other experiences can offer. It is also one of the best methods of sharpening your intuitive abilities. Becoming a Tarot reader assures that your life will be more interesting. It is a certain way to achieve personal growth, increase your enjoyment of life, and feel more fully alive.

Another benefit of becoming a good reader is an increase in self-esteem. You gain self-respect from having successfully learned to become a reader, and savor the personal satisfaction that comes from being able to advise and entertain people with your readings. When you greet new clients who were referred to you by other clients, you will take justifiable pride in your demonstrated abilities.

The benefit of increased popularity is important to some readers. Many people consider a Tarot reader to be a person worth knowing, someone they can recommend to others, and talk about to their friends and acquaintances. Readers are often in demand for various social events. Visitors may come from out of town to avail themselves of your services, and tell others about you when they return home.

Although Tarot reading should be viewed primarily as entertainment, you can and should earn money or other worthwhile compensation for your time and expertise. This compensation may be of little importance to you, or may be of substantial value. In any case, the benefits from becoming a reader are numerous and worthwhile.

A Tarot reading consists of information provided to a client by the card reader. The information is usually about the life issues or concerns of the client. The reader follows a process of laying out the cards from a Tarot deck in a pattern that is called a spread or layout. The reader then provides information based on the his or her ability to read the cards.

This ability includes knowing the meanings of each card and the significance of each position in the layout. Each card has one or more separate meanings, while each layout position pertains to some aspect of the client's life. The combination of the card meanings and the position meanings is then used by the reader to describe the circumstances, persons, and events in the client's past, present, or future. The reader combines all of these indications into one coherent presentation that should be interesting to the client and could quite possibly provide valuable information in the process.

Only the client can determine the usefulness of the information received. No reader can guarantee the accuracy of any or all the information presented in any particular reading. Therefore, the commonsense approach to Tarot reading is to regard it as something that primarily entertains the client. The reading may also yield a different perspective on events and activities in the client's personal life. Any information regarding the future should be considered as possible rather than probable. The reading is a combination of knowledge, ability, reasoning, intuition, speculation, and storytelling. The intent is not to mystify or amaze the client but to present information that is interesting, entertaining, and possibly useful in understanding his or her life situation.

Almost anyone who is interested in becoming a Tarot reader can learn to do it. Tarot reading is not a magical ability that only certain people have. The ability is learned, just as someone learns to play a musical instrument, ride a bicycle, play a game, or drive a car. It merely requires a certain amount of study and practice. Like any other learning experience, the amount of time that the process takes depends upon the individual's interest, attention, and commitment. No unusual talent is required.

The person who wishes to become a reader will need to obtain a Tarot deck, learn the meanings assigned to the cards, learn the meanings of the positions in a layout, and practice giving readings. Learning the card meanings requires memorization, just as learning the alphabet does. There are 26 letters in the alphabet and 78 cards in the Tarot deck. The memorization may seem difficult as first but it becomes easier with practice, especially if the student memorizes only a few meanings at one time. Associating meanings with the symbols on the cards is another way of learning what works well in combination with memorization. Once the meanings have been internalized, the reader will possess knowledge that will last for a lifetime. This expertise will bring personal growth and reward as well as satisfaction for your clients. *Common Sense Tarot* and any Tarot deck are all you need to become a practicing Tarot reader.

Tarot decks are sold in some shops and bookstores, and by mail order. There are a multitude of decks from which to choose, of widely differing designs and sizes. One of the most important criteria in choosing a deck is whether or not the pictures, symbols, and other information on the cards strongly appeal to you as the potential reader. You should definitely respond to and enjoy the visual impression made upon you by the cards. You should select your deck with the same care that you use in picking out any important personal possession.

All bona fide Tarot decks consist of 78 cards divided into two sets called the Minor Arcana and the Major Arcana. Arcana means secrets. The secrets are the meanings of the cards, which are known to the reader through a book of instructions such as this one. The meanings are interpreted for the client during a reading. The secrets are open in the sense that they are accessible to anyone who cares to study them.

The Minor Arcana consists of 56 cards, which are divided into four suits of 14 cards each, similar to those used in ordinary card games. Each Minor Arcana suit contains 10 pip cards numbered from ace to 10, and four face cards called the court cards, which are traditionally identified as page, knight, queen, and king. Each card bears its characteristic identifying symbols on the face side, just as in playing cards. The traditional names of the four suits are Pentacles, Cups, Swords, and Wands. Some decks may have other, slightly different names for these suits, but they are rarely confusing.

Every Minor Arcana card is identified by a symbol of the suit to which it belongs. For example, the Ace of Cups has one cup on its face side, the 2 of Cups has two cups, and so on up through the 10 of Cups. Each one of the four court cards of Cups—page, knight, queen, and king—also has a cup on the front side.

Within the Minor Arcana section:
> • The ace to 10 cards represent activities, feelings, conditions, and other aspects of life.
> • The court cards usually represent people in the client's life.

Each Minor Arcana suit is identified with a certain area of life.
> • Pentacles are associated with the physical world.
> • Cups are associated with emotions.
> • Swords are associated with mental activity.
> • Wands are associated with the spirit and motivating forces.

Unlike playing cards, the numbered cards of a Minor Arcana suit may or may not have pictures on their front side, depending on the deck. These pictures include the symbol of the suit and other details that help the reader to recall and understand the meaning of the card.

The Major Arcana consists of 22 pictorial cards that are numbered from 0 to 21 in Arabic numbers, or blank (sometimes 0) to XXI in Roman numerals. Each card of the Major Arcana represents a person, force, element, or circumstance of human existence. The Major Arcana cards are considered more powerful and more important than the

Minor Arcana cards. The Major Arcana can be considered as a larger, separate suit in which each card is a trump card. When a large number of Major Arcana cards appear in a reading, it generally means that archetypal forces are at play in the client's life situation. That is why most students of Tarot start by learning the meanings of the Major Arcana cards.

Every new Tarot deck usually comes with a brochure or book of instructions. These vary greatly in the meanings assigned to their cards and to the layouts they describe. The originator of any particular deck assigns meanings to the cards based upon tradition and then modified by personal experience, beliefs, and ideas. This may come as a disappointment to potential readers who might expect each card to have a meaning that is valid and true for all time. This is not the case. Tarot reading is a flexible system that has adapted and changed, just as human cultures and civilizations have adapted and changed over periods of time.

Some originators of Tarot decks have grafted onto the cards belief systems that were previously not associated with the Tarot deck. One of these belief systems is Astrology. Some instruction books define the characteristics of people represented by the cards in astrological terms. For this information to be most useful, both reader and client must be believers in Astrology and must believe in the same approach to Astrology as the originator of the instruction book. Since there are several systems of Astrology and disagreement from one to another, the beginning reader might well avoid such decks or ignore the astrological information. Another belief system that some originators have grafted onto the Tarot deck is the Kabbala, a system of magic based on the link between numbers and letters of the Hebrew alphabet. In this century, one Tarot deck originator switched two Major Arcana cards (numbers 8 and 11) to make the Major Arcana conform to the Hebrew alphabet and the Kabbalistic system of magic as practiced by members of the Order of the Golden Dawn. Most, if not all, beginning Tarot readers can best develop their abilities as readers if they do not burden themselves with learning or using belief systems that are inherently foreign to the Tarot. Readings that reference Astrology, the Kabbala, the Golden Dawn magical system, Jungian archetypes, or any other extraneous belief system will alienate some clients. Use of these references can also limit the reader's progress in developing an individual style of reading that communicates the maximum useful information to the client regardless of the client's belief systems. The purpose of a reading is to provide information to the client, not to change or challenge the client's belief systems or to impress the client with the reader's knowledge of various belief systems.

To understand why the meanings of the cards vary from one author to another, it is helpful to examine the history of Tarot cards. Their exact origin is not known. History consists of written records, and it seems that no one wrote down when the first Tarot deck was created. Various writers have assigned the origin of Tarot cards to Eastern and Middle Eastern civilizations but there is no definitive evidence proving any of these assertions. However, the lack of a provable origin for Tarot cards presents no handicap in using them. Their value has been demonstrated by centuries of use in a variety of cultures.

The New Columbia Encyclopedia describes Tarot cards as cards used mainly for fortune-telling, generally believed to have been brought to Western Europe by the Gypsies in the mid-fifteenth century. Virtually all authorities agree that the cards eventually became very popular. In the early bursts of popularity, various printers would create plates to print new decks each time interest resurfaced in Tarot readings. Each printer would hire a designer with some knowledge of Tarot cards to make the plates. The designer would frequently work from an existing deck and make minor variations with changes, additions, and omissions. This process has continued over the centuries and explains in part why the cards have few unchanging meanings. This is not a cause for regret. On the contrary, it is this flexibility of Tarot card meanings that has made them applicable to present-day situations.

In fact, each Tarot card means what the individual reader decides that it means. This subjective factor allows each reader to develop a personal style based on the evolving meanings of particular cards in a particular deck.

All the various decks have individual characteristics as well as different symbols on the cards. Those decks that reflect the people and symbols of medieval Europe may or may not seem appropriate to the reader who is aware of today's mixed ethnic and multi-cultural societies. So many decks bear symbols and scenes from the Middle Ages because that was when Tarot cards first gained wide popularity. Many of today's designers of Tarot decks use medieval scenes in order to appear traditional. Other decks like the Xultun Tarot and the Native American Tarot invite the reader to interpret the symbols of Mayan and American Indians, respectively. Some of the more modern decks are cosmopolitan in appearance, including symbols and people from a variety of cultures. Literally hundreds of different decks are available, which together interpret a myriad of cultural backgrounds. Some recent decks even include symbols of technological civilization such as automobiles instead of chariots, telephones instead of written messages, and computers instead of quills dipped in ink.

Colors vary greatly from deck to deck, with some available in black and white only to be colored by their owners if desired. One popular design convention is to use four different background colors for the Minor Arcana cards, one for each of the four suits. This is to remind the reader that each Minor Arcana suit represents a different aspect of life, traditionally defined as the physical, emotional, intellectual, and spiritual. Green is often used as the background for the suit of Pentacles, symbolizing the fertileness of the physical earth. Blue, suggesting water, is used to symbolize the flow of emotions in the emotional suit of Cups. Yellow, associated with mental activity in various traditions, is used for the intellectual suit of Swords. Red, associated with the spiritual fire that burns within, is thus used as the background in the spiritual suit of Wands.

A deck with color-coded backgrounds for its Minor Arcana cards allows the reader to look at a layout and immediately know what areas of the client's life are reflected in the reading. Color coding allows the reader to get this information easily, often in a single glance. Otherwise, the reader can count the Minor Arcana cards in each suit by simply looking at the symbols on the cards in the layout. This information provides a framework for making a more cohesive and focused reading.

The Major Arcana cards generally have their respective numbers 0 to 21 (0 to XXI) printed on them in Arabic (or Roman) numerals, which assists the reader in learning their assigned or traditional meanings. Most decks print the name of the card, such as The Lovers, or Strength, or The World, on the face of the card. The printed names can of course help the beginning reader attach meanings to the cards.

Some modern decks such as the Voyager Tarot give even more help to the reader by printing information on every card. The Voyager Major Arcana cards each bear the number and name of the card on its face. The Voyager Minor Arcana, which are not color-coded, identify each card with an identifier, such as Seven of Wands, and a word or phrase memory clue to meaning, such as Courage. These memory clues are helpful to the reader and also reassure a client that the meaning given to the card by the reader has a solid basis. Clients are pleased when they can see a relation between the cards and the words used in the reading. If there are no words on the card, the reader can associate the symbols on the cards with the meanings. For example, you might tell the client that the vehicle on The Chariot card indicates movement, or that the figures on The Lovers card represent a union of opposites in the life of the client.

Tarot cards, unlike regular playing cards, cannot be reversed without appearing to be upside down. In a reading, a card is considered reversed if it faces the client instead of the reader. The reader should not make any effort to assure that all cards are right-side up, as these reversals change the meaning of the card. Therefore, card reversals should be allowed to happen naturally in the shuffling of the deck.

Many authors list different meanings for reversed cards, which may require more memorization by the potential reader. A simpler, commonsense approach is to consider that any reversed card has a diminished meaning or a lesser effect. If a card with the basic meaning of reward is reversed, the reversed meaning becomes a lesser reward. If a card with the meaning of confusion is reversed, the reversed meaning becomes less confusion or possibly an end to confusion. This system for determining the meaning of reversed cards is used by many readers even when not mentioned in the instructions for a particular deck.

The potential reader should consider all Tarot instructions as a guide by which the reader travels an individual path toward the goal of becoming an interesting, entertaining, and effective reader. All meanings are determined by the reader within the context of the layout and the particular reading. Likewise, the position of any card in the layout is just as important as the meaning of the card itself. Each reader is entitled to use the meanings, layouts, and cards in any way that develops a unique, personal style of reading. The reader becomes his or her own authority and demonstrates this authority in readings.

The information in the reading comes not only from the reader's memory of the cards and the positions of the layout. The reader also uses whatever information is available from any source. For example, if the reader is well acquainted with the client, a mutually known incident in the client's past may lead the reader to compare the present situation with the client's life at that previous time. Do not take the attitude that all information discussed must come from the cards, thereby ignoring other valuable sources.

Other personal information about the client can be incorporated into the reading as appropriate. Just seeing the client gives the reader important information about dress, appearance, and manner. Hearing the client speak gives the reader information about accent, language, word choice, and attitude. All of this information should enter the reader's rational mode of consciousness, which is the linear and logical way.

The reader also uses the intuitive mode of consciousness, which Tarot reading helps develop more fully. Intuition is immediate comprehension not based on rational or logical thought. The intuitive mode of consciousness is concerned with knowledge based on perceptions that are largely ignored by the rational mode of consciousness. The intuitive mode operates receptively and holistically. There is nothing inherently mystical, occult-like, or psychic about the process of intuition. This mode of consciousness becomes more accessible as the individual learns to recognize it and to pay attention to it.

Most people, whether they are Tarot readers or not, have intuitive experiences.

Some common ones are:
- Hearing the telephone ring when no call is expected and being certain who is calling,
- Perceiving something without awareness of rational thought about it, such as realizing someone is married or pregnant or undergoing an unexpected change,
- Realizing that an impromptu visit to friends is intrusive, although neither their actions nor speech indicate it,
- Expecting to find a parking place in a congested area and then driving directly to it,
- Feeling under observation and confirming it by a quick look over the shoulder.

Similar intuitive experiences occur among people in all cultures even if the culture doesn't emphasize the importance of intuition. Cultures often devalue intuitive information because the rational mode of consciousness is considered more important to individual survival and cultural continuance. Intuitive information is often the most exciting part of a Tarot reading, sometimes making the client suspect that the reader has paranormal powers.

Some readers claim such powers, asserting that their systems of reference and belief provide them with information from occult or unknown sources. Such claims and beliefs are not necessary to a successful Tarot reader. The commonsense approach emphasizes that the information comes from the mind of the reader. There are many ways in which that information is generated. What is important to the client is the reading. The reader should not detract from the reading by explaining any personal theories or beliefs unless the client needs that information to feel comfortable with the reading. The reader should be especially careful to avoid detailed explanations of systems that may be foreign to the client's beliefs. For example, a client who considers Astrology to be nonsense may well consider a reading couched in zodiacal references to be nonsense also.

The procedure for a reading is simple. The reader shuffles the deck at least seven times, which is the number of shuffles required to remove any existing pattern according to principles of mathematical randomization. The client then cuts the cards or touches one from a spread-out, face-down deck, signifying the beginning of the deal. This is the personal touch that assures the client that he or she has directly influenced the cards. The touched card or the card on top of the cut becomes the first card of the layout for the client.

The reader deals the cards into a chosen layout in the proper order. Selected layouts are presented in Chapters 9 through 13 of this book. Other layouts are usually described in the instructions that accompany any Tarot deck. The reader then looks at the cards as if they are telling a story. The central character of the story is the client, and the narrative represents a part of the client's life. Each card in each position is an element of the story as determined by the meaning of the card and the significance of the position. The reader becomes a storyteller, supplying the words that connect all the meanings into an informative, entertaining tale about the client. The process becomes easier as the reader gains experience in cohesive storytelling. Every reading helps the new reader to gain confidence and develop an individual style.

In summary, a Tarot reading consists of information about a client which is interpreted by a reader. A person becomes a Tarot reader by obtaining a Tarot deck, learning the meanings associated with the cards, and learning various layouts. Each layout is a system of dealing the cards into certain positions in a prescribed order. Each position has a meaning. The combination of the meanings of the cards and the meanings of the layout positions yields the information upon which the reading is based. There is nothing necessarily psychic, occult-like, or magical about a Tarot reading. Almost anyone can become a Tarot reader if he or she is willing to spend the time necessary to learn the card meanings and layout positions.

Learning the Meanings of the Cards

After the potential reader has obtained a deck of Tarot cards, the next step in becoming a reader is learning the meanings of the cards. This requires memorization work. There is no way to avoid it. Just as an actor must learn the lines of the play for performing on-stage, the potential Tarot reader must learn the meanings of all the cards in order to do a reading.

This is the most time-consuming part of the reader's preparation, but it is not difficult for anyone who is motivated. Everyone has memorized a great deal of information in the process of becoming an adult. Just as a teacher learns the names of students, the potential reader learns the meanings of the cards as they become more and more familiar with repeated exposure. The potential reader will learn to recognize the faces of the cards, and visual recognition will automatically supply the meanings that have been studied.

The memorization process will be effort well-expended. The value of memorization cannot be overemphasized. While it is possible to give a Tarot reading by using a book to look up the meaning of each card in a selected layout, the resulting reading will be choppy and disconnected—perhaps even incoherent. Such a reading can be a useful learning exercise but is quite unsatisfactory for any client who expects to receive useful information about what is occurring in his or her life. The proficiency gained through memorization is necessary to satisfy the client and to appear capable.

There are numerous approaches to learning the meanings. In some localities, teachers of Tarot offer classes for potential readers. Most likely there will be a number of students, and the teacher may specify which Tarot deck the student should use in class. The teacher usually bases the instruction on his or her personal knowledge of several decks of Tarot cards. Although this gives the potential reader a narrower choice in the initial deck used, the reader can later select another deck if desired. Most readers have more than one Tarot deck and use whichever one they or the client prefers for a reading.

The teacher in a Tarot class helps each student learn to associate particular meanings with each card. Some teachers start by asking students what the pictures and symbols on the cards mean to them individually. Other teachers will require the students to learn the meanings given in the deck instructions, or in one or more recommended Tarot textbooks such as this one. The teacher may or may not follow the information in the deck instructions, these being merely a point of departure. The instruction is more likely to be based on the teacher's considerable personal experience in reading the cards.

Most teachers emphasize that there is no one correct meaning or set of meanings for any particular card. The student is urged to become so familiar with the cards that one or more meanings become associated with each card in the student's deck. The meanings discussed in the class by the teacher are often just a convenience for the student. The student will eventually learn that as an accomplished reader; whichever meanings come unbidden to the mind when the card is first seen are the ones to be included and referred to in any particular reading. This phenomenon is an indication to the reader that the extensive memory work has paid off. The reader now has meanings automatically accessible through memory.

A Tarot teacher will also discuss many other things that a student needs to know in order to become a fully developed reader. This kind of information will be covered in subsequent chapters of this book. This chapter concentrates on the importance of learning meanings as an essential step in becoming an effective reader. The meanings can be learned with or without a teacher. Some students might learn faster in a class; others might learn better by individual study.

Since the 22 cards of the Major Arcana are the most important cards in the Tarot deck, they are a good place to start learning card meanings. These 22 cards identify major aspects of the human condition. They are as important to Tarot readings as trumps in an ordinary card game.

Separate the Major Arcana cards from the rest of the deck and look at them carefully. Examine each card to determine what symbols and images it uses. Learn the names of these cards, and associate their names with their images so that you immediately recognize each Major Arcana card when it appears.

The names of all 22 Major Arcana cards do not have to be learned all at once or at a single sitting. Feel free to set your own pace for learning, compatible with your abilities and time schedule. Once the names of the Major Arcana cards have been learned, then start associating meanings with the names and faces of these cards. Look at each card and then read the meanings associated with it as listed in this book or the deck instructions. Reading the meanings aloud while looking at the cards is a useful technique because words heard will often be better remembered than words read silently.

Once the meanings begin to seem familiar, concentrate on connecting meanings to the first five cards of the Major Arcana. Separate these cards from the rest and then reread the meanings associated with them while looking at each card in turn. Examine each card and see which meanings can be associated with the face of the card. Write these meanings in this book, in the instruction book, or in a separate notebook. If the card seems to have a distinct meaning, or one not listed elsewhere, write down that meaning for possible future use.

The time required to learn meanings for the five cards will vary with each individual, so it need not be done in any particular time frame. It doesn't matter whether it takes a day, a week, or longer. Once the significant meanings of the first five cards of the Major Arcana have been checked, marked, or written down, then do the same with the next six cards. Repeat the process with the next five and then the next six cards until all 22 of them have some meaning connected in memory to their names and faces. Carefully examine the meanings you have written down. Make certain that you understand them in a manner that leads to easy memorization. If the meanings seem too complex, simplify them for easier memorization.

After marking or writing down meanings for all the Major Arcana cards, these meanings must be memorized. There is no hurry about this. Take the necessary time as it is available and convenient. Students who are accustomed to memorization may already have techniques of particular use to them. However, here are several general techniques that can aid the memorization process for almost anyone.

One memorization technique is to shuffle the Major Arcana cards and then deal out five or six of them face up. Then recite aloud the memorized meanings associated with each card. This checks the memory against the marked or written list. Put aside those that you remember correctly. Now shuffle those that were not remembered into the remaining Major Arcana cards, and repeat the process. Continue this procedure until all cards have been examined at least once. Repeat this technique as many times as possible. If you repeatedly associate a card with a meaning that is not marked or listed, write down this meaning because it represents what that card means to you. If it is a meaning traditionally associated with another card, resolve the issue in any way that fits with your style and memory.

After acquiring a good working knowledge of meanings for the Major Arcana, the Minor Arcana can be approached one suit at a time. Since the four suits deal with separate areas of human existence, you might elect to start with the suit that interests you the most. Or begin with any suit that seems easier to memorize than the others. The suits do not have to be learned in any particular sequence.

After selecting which suit to examine first, separate that suit from the rest of the deck. Then read the given meanings for all the cards in that suit. Examine each card carefully so you will recognize the symbols and information on the cards.

Bear in mind that the numbered cards pertain to certain aspects of life associated with that suit. The court cards represent individuals with characteristics pertaining to those aspects of life, usually other people involved in the client's life.

One recommended procedure for learning the Minor Arcana meanings is to study the ace through 5 first, the 6 through 10 next, and then the four court cards. Record the meanings in this book, in the deck instructions, or in a separate notebook. Study the meanings in whatever way is effective. The same techniques that produced results in learning meanings for the Major Arcana can be used for all four suits of the Minor Arcana.

After determining meanings for all 78 cards to your satisfaction, continue the memorization process until all the cards are familiar. However, do not limit yourself to the memorization techniques given here. The help of a friend or the use of a tape recorder might be very helpful. Any technique that may produce results is worth trying. Once memorization is relatively complete, the hardest part of the preparations for becoming a reader is over.

3

The Major Arcana

This chapter provides the meanings of the 22 Major Arcana cards. The meanings listed here are not the only possible meanings. They are a composite list adapted from a number of books, instructions, and readers. Some of the meanings are old and traditional; others are new and reflect the knowledge and insights of modern-day Tarot designers and readers.

The names assigned to the Major Arcana here are traditional. They will not exactly match those in some decks, especially those of recent design. You should, nevertheless, have no difficulty in identifying which Major Arcana card in any deck is associated with the meanings given here. The assigned name or number may just be different. For example, some decks identify Major Arcanum 5 as The High Priest or The Pope instead of The Hierophant. The listed meanings still apply because these different titles all denote a spiritual leader, which is the unique attribute of this particular card in all decks.

Do not consider any one particular meaning essential to an understanding of Tarot reading. When the reader has a Tarot deck, each of the Major Arcana cards should be examined in relation to these meanings and/or to the meanings given in the instructions that accompany the deck. The easiest procedure is for the potential reader to mark down one major meaning. Pick a particular meaning that seems to have a good connection in your mind to the symbols and pictures on that card. The record could be written in this book, in the instructions that accompany the deck, or in a notebook for reference. The important thing to remember is that each individual card has the meaning that the reader assigns to it. The reader is the final authority on the meaning of any card at any time.

0—THE FOOL

Some Tarot decks designate The Fool card as number 22 (or XXII) instead of number 0. The Fool, by either number, still has the same meanings for the reader.

The Fool card represents a person who has a childlike quality of innocence, who can relax and play in the world. He or she is open to new experiences and eager to discover the best in others and in the world. The Fool is ready to begin or continue the journey of discovery, possibly in a new or different direction.

The Fool signifies the essence of life with all its dualities and possibilities. He or she symbolizes the common state of every person, a combination of knowledge and ignorance, a mixture of playfulness and seriousness. The Fool is in touch with his or her individual potential.

In a reading, depending on the position in which The Fool card appears, it frequently represents the client or another person who may affect the client's life.

Possible meanings are:
- Going on a journey,
- Discovering something new,
- Taking chances,
- Turning experience into wisdom,
- Exploring the spirit of life.

1—THE MAGICIAN

The Magician card represents a person with power and talent, who knows how to work creatively within the framework of his or her own limitations. He or she is open to whatever opportunities exist and is able to use them. The magician symbolizes the ability to utilize inner resources to achieve aspirations.

The Magician acts and operates in the physical world, which is his main concern. This card, like other cards in the Major Arcana that represent people, may signify either the client or a person who has an influence on the client.

The Magician card represents the abilities to cheer people, to cure them, to communicate powerful ideas, and to help people learn about themselves. It can also represent trickery or deceit.

Possible meanings are:
- Opportunity utilized,
- Power,
- Talent,
- Benefits,
- Trickery or deceit, revealed or concealed.

2—THE HIGH PRIESTESS

The High Priestess card represents the nurturing of potential. She intuitively knows what others need to grow and develop. She has knowledge, wisdom, and perceptions that can easily be brought to influence the material world. She symbolizes consciousness and all principles identified as feminine.

The High Priestess is calm and emotionally self-sufficient. Her wisdom gives her balance, and comes from her dreams and meditations. She attempts, usually successfully, to remain free of any attachment, emotional or physical, that might disturb the completeness and purity of her vision. She is contemplative and spiritual. Her aspirations are balanced and she understands emotions.

In a reading The High Priestess card can represent the client, the female aspect of the client, or an influence on the client.

Possible meanings are:
- Nurturing,
- Giving,
- Raising consciousness,
- Emotional balance,
- Wisdom.

3—THE EMPRESS

The Empress card is the female authority figure who symbolizes protection and preservation. She is creative and has the ability to revive, resurrect, and reconstruct. She uses her powers wisely and with great practicality.

The Empress represents the earth-mother who loves and feels compassion for all the creatures of the earth without being overly judgmental in spirit or action. She is fruitful and provides abundance, sometimes in a very pragmatic way. Often she is concerned more with the group than its individual members.

Those who want the total attention of The Empress for extended periods of time will be disappointed. She intends to deal fairly with everyone in an open manner. The Empress card can indicate the overcoming of a shallow and possessive inclination.

Possible meanings are:
- Fertility,
- Abundance,
- Protection,
- Preservation,
- Shallowness and possessiveness overcome.

4—THE EMPEROR

The Emperor card is the male authority figure responsible for making things work efficiently and correctly in the physical world. He is organized and believes strongly in organizations with firm structures. He is the ultimate leader, the leader of other leaders.

The Emperor is an initiator, an active empire-builder who trusts his judgment and common sense. He has a large ego that may cause him to be overly competitive in his drive for personal wealth and professional recognition.

The Emperor expects everyone over whom he has power to follow his rules. He allows little room for individual initiative on the part of those he considers his followers or underlings. His tendency is to stifle individuals whose talents and abilities he does not consider useful to him. He has little use for spontaneity in himself or others.

Possible meanings are:
- Authority,
- Organizational ability,
- Decisiveness,
- Compulsion to achieve,
- Lack of spontaneity.

5—THE HIEROPHANT

The Hierophant card is the high priest and represents the spiritual world as understood by the intellect. He has large inner resources. He has power and authority based on his position in the realm of spirituality.

The Hierophant has attained this position through study. The Hierophant is aware of the old traditions. If he has accepted them in blind faith and believes they are of universal value, he is hampered by dogma and inflexibility.

The Hierophant wants to help people and show that he cares for them. His advice is always well-meant but it may be limited in value by his faith in the dominant religion of his culture. If he has overcome the cultural trance that says there is only one way to view reality, then he has attained cultural and spiritual mastery.

In a reading this card may signify an outside spiritual force, or it may represent the beliefs, morals, and ethics of the client.

Possible meanings are:
- Spiritual growth,
- Informed advice,
- Ethical awareness,
- Inflexibility,
- Culture shock.

6—THE LOVERS

The Lovers card represent the union of opposites. It refers to the emotional growth that is necessary for shared human activity in a committed relationship. This voluntary sharing, influenced by sexual desire and emotional needs, is an effective way for the individual to transcend the view of the physical self as separate from others and from the rest of the world. Lovers know that they are not separate from the world but connected to all of it through each other.

The Lovers card symbolizes a romantic joining in which the individuals go beyond the fantasies of the culture and the limited sexual roles superficially represented in their society. Successful lovers in their emotional partnering achieve a harmony of their inner and outer lives that allows them to transcend many perils and pitfalls.

Possible meanings are:
- Union of opposites,
- Emotional growth,
- Romance,
- Harmony,
- Correct choice made.

7—THE CHARIOT

The Chariot card represents movement in life and its accompanying physical changes. It reflects the continuing motion of the earth and the principle of expansion in the individual's life.

The movement of The Chariot can be via travel, relocation, or extension of the environment. Although this can result in emotional, spiritual, or intellectual growth, the predominant concern is with the physical world. The individual is in charge of this motion even if he or she is not the sole initiator of the forces involved. Although the changes may be rapid, they are not beyond control of the person involved.

The illusion of staying in one place has been dispelled. The forces are in motion that will bring the individual to a better place.

Possible meanings are:
- Travel,
- Physical changes in residence,
- Goals approached,
- Getting things done,
- Renewed vigor.

8—JUSTICE

(NOTE: This card is numbered 11 in some decks that deviate from the older Tarot tradition, and identify the Strength card as number 8.)

The card of Justice represents the effort to restore balance and harmony in the world with fairness. Justice has the necessary force to endure and proceed in efforts to restore equilibrium. It sees all sides of the issue with objectivity and is blind to subjectivity. Justice is impartial and impersonal because its decisions are concerned with the circumstances and the rules, not with the personalities involved.

Justice requires the taking of responsibility and making of decisions. It requires that the individual take responsibility for his or her actions, correctly seeing irresponsibility as guilt. When the individual exercises freedom without assuming the responsibility for it, Justice steps in to limit freedom until responsibility is learned. Justice sees guilt as the failure to act responsibly.

Possible meanings are:
- Balance,
- Harmony,
- Impersonal forces,
- Decisions,
- Responsibility.

9—THE HERMIT

The Hermit card minimizes worldly distractions in an effort to realize a wider objective. This objective is the formulation of a personal philosophy that embraces both the physical and spiritual aspects of existence. The objective is approached by a partial withdrawal from the world so that wisdom can be gained through solitude and silence.

The Hermit signifies the inward look that must be taken after a significant period of accomplishment and development. The achievements of the past must be examined in order to determine how previous actions and events can be viewed with a perspective that embraces past, present, and future. The Hermit is self-sufficient, demanding nothing and making-do with the resources that have been accumulated and developed during a productive period. What The Hermit achieves is an increase of power and a deeper understanding of what life means.

Possible meanings are:
- Introspection,
- Re-evaluation,
- Philosophical understanding,
- Spiritual development,
- Wisdom.

10—FORTUNE

The Fortune card represents a constantly-spinning wheel of life, which brings prosperity and a wealth of opportunities for greater expansion and flexibility. The individual who relies on more than just luck will find favorable conditions to help recycle the wealth of the physical world.

Fortune may well involve activities connected to speculation, but not to gambling. Speculation is defined as taking a risk that already exists, while gambling is defined as taking a risk that you create.

Fortune symbolizes the acquisition of the good things of the world in return for honest, intelligent effort. A person receives Fortune not because of the feeling that he or she deserves it but because it is a return on sharing and investing.

Possible meanings are:
- Prosperity,
- Opportunities,
- Expansion,
- Greater resources,
- Sharing rewarded.

11—STRENGTH

(NOTE: In some decks that deviate from the older Tarot tradition, this card may be numbered 8 instead of 11.)

The card of Strength represents the intelligent use of your forces to achieve your purposes. The person with Strength is well-centered, has self-respect, and possesses earned confidence. This card suggests that the individual has control over mind and emotion as well as physical resources.

Strength symbolizes the enduring quality of the spirit, a sense of permanence, and an awareness of the eternal. The person with these qualities is able to maintain balance and equilibrium, achieving reasonableness even when outside pressures seem unreasonable. Reasonableness is characteristic of the person who is secure in the knowledge of his or her own strong resources. If the person lacks reasonableness, the danger of Strength is a desire for control that wastes inner resources through domination, intimidation, and oppression.

Possible meanings are:
- Strength,
- Self-esteem,
- Resources,
- Balance,
- Control.

12—THE HANGED MAN

The Hanged Man card does not represent someone being executed, but a person who is in a hung-up condition. It suggests a period in a person's life in which nothing seems to change. It does not mean that conditions are bad. The existing conditions, regardless of whatever they are, seem inclined to endure for awhile longer. The person must be patient. If good conditions exist, they should be affirmed. Actions should be taken to maintain life as it is. Bad conditions can be mitigated by the awareness that this is the state prior to the emergence of a feeling of renewal.

The Hanged Man is stationary. Little movement is possible, and no change or expansion can come soon. The forces that have produced this environmental limbo are beyond the control of the individual. This is the time to develop patience, to accept what is instead of what might have been or what may be someday.

Possible meanings are:
> • Stagnation,
> • Requirement for patience,
> • Acceptance of the present,
> • No impending changes,
> • A calm preceding a storm.

13—DEATH

The card of Death signifies an abrupt change that has not been anticipated. Rarely does this card refer to physical death. Instead it signifies the impermanence of all things, reminding us that everything changes with the passage of time. Death symbolizes a great change that is coming soon. If anticipated, it is not the change to which this card refers.

Death symbolizes the process that allows the new to flourish when the old is gone. Old habits must vanish if new habits are to be put in their place. If everything were permanent, there would be no movement. This card represents a movement that comes as a surprise, something so unexpected that there can be no preparation. It symbolizes irreversible change in thinking, experiencing, or existing. Because the individual is not alerted to it, it brings startling surprise.

Possible meanings are:
> • Abrupt change,
> • Unexpected change,
> • Impermanence,
> • Reorientation,
> • An ending.

14—TEMPERANCE

Temperance is the card of reasonableness, of avoiding

excesses that can damage the quality of life. It is the card of moderation, indicating neither addiction or abstinence. Temperance is created by internal balance, reflected by consideration for others as well as for self.

Temperance is the middle way, a point of reasonableness between the extremes. The person to whom Temperance refers is aware of the value of compromise. An unwillingness to compromise under any circumstances is alien to this card. Temperance comes from the emotional and intellectual maturity that recognizes the value of others and avoids damaging actions. Temperance indicates that an active intelligence is involved in emotional matters.

Possible meanings are:
- Reasonableness,
- Moderation,
- Emotional balance,
- Active intelligence,
- Avoidance of extremes.

15—THE DEVIL

The Devil card represents denial, lack of recognition, lack of acceptance, and unintelligent extremes. It suggests a failure to recognize that good and evil are abstract terms based on individual judgment. The Devil tries to avoid individual responsibility. The Devil assigns unpleasant or unpopular thoughts, feelings, and actions onto someone or something else, instead of admitting that these come from within oneself.

The Devil symbolizes unethical and unintelligent behavior such as prejudice, dishonesty, bigotry, chauvinism, and mindless persecution. All of these behaviors have unpleasant consequences for both the initiators of such actions and those who experience or perceive the results. The irony of such ignorance in action is that it damages both the actors and those acted upon. The damage to the victims is often more apparent but the perpetrators are likewise diminished. They allow all that The Devil represents to live in their minds and bodies until they learn to think and act with kindness and understanding.

Possible meanings are:
- Dishonesty,
- Bigotry,
- Ignorance,
- Chauvinism,
- Prejudice.

16—THE TOWER

The Tower card signifies great change in the life of the individual. New inputs or insights reveal that the structure created from belief and understood experience is being changed whether the individual is ready or not. The Tower symbolizes this structure. The card shows that the structure will never be the same.

The Tower represents a deep, radical mental reorientation as the result of spiritual, religious, or occult perceptions. Neither the reorientation nor the perceptions have been sought. They are part of a chain of circumstances that will alter the way the individual experiences the world. This alteration is mental rather than physical and may be difficult and demanding, requiring courage and strength.

The Tower portrays a restructuring that involves the discarding of inappropriate defenses. Chaos and confusion last until the liberating reorientation becomes solid.

Possible meanings are:
- Sudden change in personal belief structure,
- Involuntary mental reorientation,
- Permanent perceptual change,
- Need for courage and strength,
- Chaos preceding liberation.

17—THE STAR

The Star card represents the enlightenment that brings a meaningful personal knowledge of reality. Each person lives in a separate reality created by the mind as it filters, classifies, and packages the input from experience and from thought. The recognition that the individual can take responsibility for this process is symbolized by the light of The Star.

The Star signifies productive and progressive mental growth accompanied by optimism, hope, excitement, and aspiration. A great increase in compassion is in process. New understanding leads the way to a greater comprehension and an increased appreciation of ideals.

The individual now glows with an inner light. Anything is seen to be possible. The light of The Star illuminates both the mental and spiritual landscapes. An increase in trust allows the individual to identify with all of humanity.

Possible meanings are:
- Enlightenment,
- Mental growth,
- Increased compassion,
- Greater trust,
- Identification with all of humanity.

18—THE MOON

The Moon card reminds us that cycles in all things are part of a natural order. Knowledge of such patterns of gradual change facilitates emotional maturity and greater harmony in life. The continuity of transformation perpetually creates new beginnings as the present is gently replaced by the future.

The Moon also symbolizes the light that guides during the night and illuminates the theater of dreams. It is the light of intuition that blesses us with greater awareness and acceptance of events, people, and activities.

The Moon also indicates a time when old relationships and emotional attachments enter into a new phase that reflects increasing emotional maturity.

Possible meanings are:
- Cycles of gradual change,
- Prophetic dreams,
- Increased intuition,
- Evolving relationships,
- Emotional maturity.

19—THE SUN

The Sun card symbolizes what is essential to life. The brilliant energy of this card is an omen of good things in combination—health, awareness, productivity, harmony, and realization of material goals. All the positive things associated with sunshine are symbolized here. The Sun indicates that good fortune in its many aspects is shining down. It predicts that things will go smoothly and swiftly in the desired direction.

The Sun banishes fears that are associated with forces of darkness. It creates a feeling of expansiveness. Goals seem within reach, and aspirations are prelude to achievement. The energy of The Sun seeks to unify the body, mind, and spirit.

The Sun is a harbinger of harmony in both work and play, expanding consciousness to embrace all of life.

Possible meanings are:
- Health,
- Joyful awareness,
- Productivity,
- Harmony,
- Realization of material goals.

20—JUDGMENT

The card of Judgment is concerned with understanding. Judgment indicates a time for clearing away the emotions of the past. It indicates an understanding that the past is not what is occurring now. The past is actually a thought process that is individually shaped by each person. Judgment is the time for understanding this, so as to leave the emotions of the past in order to fully experience the emotions of the present.

The understanding within the Judgment card leads to forgiveness, not only of others but of the self. Understanding is that emotional evolution of consciousness that frees the individual to move on, to accept what was and forget what might have been.

Judgment is associated with punishment and reward. The punishment comes from clinging to displaced emotions of the past. The reward comes from the emotional freedom to live in the present.

Possible meanings are:
- Emotional understanding,
- Forgiveness of self,

- Forgiveness of others,
- Acceptance of the past,
- Feeling emotional freedom.

21—THE WORLD

The World card indicates that all things in the world are possible. It is a symbol of the centered individual in the center of all things. It represents the conviction that the world is a positive framework.

The World signifies success, both in the subjective world and the objective world. The illusions of the past have been vanquished, replaced by the luck and grace that characterize new knowledge.

The World suggests that a person's challenges have been successfully mastered. The necessary lessons have been learned. The journey of discovery begun by The Fool is now complete; the individual is now able to act intelligently based on deep understanding of his or her experience. Realistic possibilities can be perceived with clarity. This is the card of wholeness.

Possible meanings are:
- Internal balance and humor,
- Being in the center of things,
- Extensive knowledge of the world,
- Success,
- Wholeness.

The Suit of Pentacles

The Minor Arcana suit traditionally called Pentacles is named for the five-pointed star that is its symbol or icon. In various Tarot decks this suit is designated as Coins, Disks, Jades, Worlds, or other names that describe a similar circular icon.

The suit of Pentacles is identified with the physical world, the things of the earth that can be seen and touched, and all that the human senses perceive. The cards in this suit are concerned with possessions, money, physical health, the body, all of the various objects in the material world, and all physical activities of any nature.

When cards from this suit predominate in a layout, it signals the reader that the information in the reading concerns the client's physical world, or actions and objects within it.

THE ACE OF PENTACLES

The 1 or Ace of Pentacles card represents prosperity, a

successful completion of physical efforts of the highest standards. It is associated with superb and enduring craftsmanship that is functional and yet appeals strongly to the senses. This physical and material prosperity may be just beginning. Its seeds, however, were planted some time ago. Full growth is now underway. Physical impediments have all been removed and the material of the earth is now available in abundance.

The Ace of Pentacles favors new business ventures. There is ample ability to provide, produce, and bring about the creation of plenty. Projects can begin on time and be completed on schedule.

The Ace of Pentacles can signify good physical health as well as good fortune. This is the card of productive physical activity, for the body is capable at this time of meeting all demands placed on it.

Possible meanings are:
- Success,
- Prosperity,
- Health,
- Abundance,
- Productive physical activity.

THE 2 OF PENTACLES

The 2 of Pentacles card represents duality. The time is one of competition, perhaps in business negotiations or in sports and games. Security and strength are required. Dangerous risks should be avoided or postponed if possible.

Times are changing and efforts should be concentrated on projects in process. Starting new ventures at this time could require more juggling of physical assets than is comfortable or reasonable. All physical and material options should be examined carefully because the future is full of uncertainty.

Physical acts undertaken at this time may be missing the emotional context necessary to make them meaningful and enjoyable. Efforts should be made to keep things as simple as possible in the physical world. This is the time to consider the possible benefits of austerity and frugality in connection with the physical world.

Possible meanings are:
- Duality,
- Competition,
- Uncertainty,
- Physical limitations,
- Austerity.

THE 3 OF PENTACLES

The 3 of Pentacles is a card of nurturing and growth. The physical actions taken thus far have been correct, and now the process must be supported to produce the desired results. Creativity will soon be rewarded if the nurturing process is continued.

Labor has been productive. The attention paid to high standards of craftsmanship is generating physical rewards. Although care must be taken to ensure the desired results, all the phases of the project so far have been successfully completed.

The probabilities of material gain and monetary reward are high. The possibility of attracting a patron or sponsor arises in the near future. This individual or group will recognize and nurture creativity while appreciating knowledge and ability.

Possible meanings are;
> • Nurturing,
> • Growth,
> • Productivity,
> • Material gain,
> • Monetary reward.

THE 4 OF PENTACLES

The 4 of Pentacles is a card that signifies new beginnings. The commencement of a new endeavor looks promising. New seeds should be sown because it is a time for planting. There are assurances that growth is a certainty.

Unexpected resources are just out of sight, but can soon be utilized. An unexpected gift or legacy may soon be delivered or discovered. Look for unanticipated benefits.

It is a time to enjoy the present and be ready for pleasant surprises. The present physical situation is propitious, and can ripen into advantage with little effort. Personal security is assured, having been established by previous actions. Confidence in all things pertaining to the senses is warranted.

Possible meanings are:
> • New beginnings,
> • A new endeavor,
> • A gift or legacy,
> • Security,
> • Confidence.

THE 5 OF PENTACLES

The 5 of Pentacles card signals the possibility of unexpected difficulties in the tangible matters. There is a potential for problems with finances, health, home, work, or possessions. Resources may become strained.

A setback in some aspect of physical reality is likely. Even the weather is apt to be unfavorable to projects undertaken or underway at this time. Unexpected events with undesirable results may occur.

A setback may end a project or task that was filled with hope—not every seed can thrive. Things grow old and die so that they can be replaced by new growth, an inescapable pattern of life. Do not mourn for what is lost; now is the time to make room for something new.

Possible meanings are:
- Unexpected difficulties,
- Setbacks,
- Unfavorable weather,
- Failure of a project,
- An end leading to a new start.

THE 6 OF PENTACLES

The 6 of Pentacles card suggests that assets from a variety of sources have come together in a bountiful way. Physical attributes from many different areas coalesce into a whole that is greater than the sum of its parts. This causes a surge of creative energy to be released.

It is a time for sharing, for giving and receiving presents, for generosity, endowments, volunteering, charity, and philanthropy in the physical world.

Resources of the individual may be combined with the resources of others to create new possibilities. Much can be achieved with cooperation and teamwork. The path is open for the achievement of major goals.

Possible meanings are:
- Combination of assets,
- Creative energy unleashed,
- Giving and receiving,
- Teamwork,
- Cooperation.

THE 7 OF PENTACLES

The 7 of Pentacles card is concerned with finances, for all matters dealing with money are influenced by it. The time of shortage has ended, and an abundant supply is indicated. The budget now allows for more than the basic necessities; some luxuries can become a reality.

The time of wanting has passed; penury and frugality are no longer appropriate. The financial house is in order. Property, real estate, and finances are easily managed. Fund-raising drives and charity events will be successful; minimum needs are more than met.

This card represents financial breakthrough, a time that has been long awaited. Look for success in business and all pecuniary matters that can be enhanced by this card.

Possible meanings are:
- More money,
- Success in business,
- Gains associated with real estate,
- Financial breakthrough,
- An end to frugality.

THE 8 OF PENTACLES

The 8 of Pentacles is the card of positive pleasure in the world of material things. Enjoyable work is going to be available. An apprenticeship is possible for the person who wishes to learn a new skill or craft. Artistic efforts will be commissioned or interesting projects offered.

The 8 of Pentacles signifies that the person's environment lends support to what is needed in the material world to foster and increase enjoyment. Physical exertion, whether in work or play, will be pleasurable and happily productive in ways that reflect a new maturity.

Completion of a cycle is implied in the aspects of this card. This is a positive sign of growth and recognized achievement. The identity of the individual is joyously confirmed.

Possible meanings are:
- Positive physical pleasure,
- Enjoyable work,
- Interesting projects,
- A supportive environment,
- Completion of a cycle.

THE 9 OF PENTACLES

The 9 of Pentacles card indicates a harvest, a time of life in which to enjoy and appreciate material success. A more leisurely pace is possible. The fruits of labors are ripe, and the physical needs of the individual can be easily met with the resources at hand.

The 9 of Pentacles symbolizes comfort. If healing of the body is needed, this card can appear here. There is a union with the environment, an integration of needs and desires that leaves the individual with time to enjoy the physical world. A greater knowledge of both cultural reality and personal reality can be experienced.

Projects can be finished, business affairs completed. The accumulated garbage of life is properly disposed of and the physical pleasures of life can be appreciated.

Possible meanings are:
- Appreciation of material success,
- Increased leisure,
- Enjoyment of the physical world,
- Projects finished,
- Business affairs completed.

THE 10 OF PENTACLES

The 10 of Pentacles card represents the completion of a major cycle of physical existence. The individual is rewarded with material success for work well-done. The rewards exceed need, and wealth is available for sharing.

This is a time of abundance that has been earned through effort and sincere application. Security is evident and assured. The energy that has been expended is converted into material prosperity.

There is a glow of satisfaction that comes with the rewards inherent in this card. The individual receives this reward not by chance but as the result of achievement, diligence, and determination. Earthly matters have all been dealt with properly and respectfully.

Possible meanings are:
- Reward,
- Material success,
- Wealth,
- Completion,
- Satisfaction.

THE PAGE OF PENTACLES

The Page of Pentacles card represents a young person, possibly a child, who has not yet been given full rights in the culture and society. He or she is an apprentice, not yet initiated into the concerns of the adult world.

The Page of Pentacles is preoccupied with fun and games that seem childish or childlike. This individual had good instincts, a vivid imagination, and strong physical resources. The need and desire for change and transformation is strong, and often affects his or her actions in predictable ways.

The person represented by this card is primarily concerned with the phenomenal world. The Page seeks someone to be a guide in the ways of worldly matters, but is drawn to and remains open to anything that is fresh and new.

Possible characteristics of this person are:
- Childlike,
- Childish,
- Little status,
- Open,
- Seeking change.

THE KNIGHT OF PENTACLES

The Knight of Pentacles card represents a person who has passed through puberty but is still young, and most likely unmarried. This youth is physically active, possibly athletic or into a regular program of intensive physical activity.

The Knight of Pentacles represents a person who is watchful without being paranoid, dependable without being obtrusive. Other probable characteristics include resourcefulness, practicality, and loyalty.

The Knight of Pentacles is an agent of physical change who has a strong drive for worldly expansiveness. He or she is open-minded, and willing to listen and absorb new ideas. This is a person deeply interested in the opinions of others who are more experienced.

Possible characteristics of this person are:
- Unmarried,
- Physically active,
- Loyal,
- Expansive,
- Willing to listen.

THE QUEEN OF PENTACLES

The Queen of Pentacles card represents a mature woman of marriageable age. She is a nurturer and provider, with great endurance. Her skills and talents suggest a superb homemaker, if that is her choice.

She believes in and strives to preserve tradition; she understands the social fabric of family and community. She exerts her energy to maintain this fabric throughout her entire life for the benefit of all involved.

She is concerned with the physical health and well-being of the family. She has nursing instincts. She is motivated by her emotions, which are the strongest influence on her many worldly actions. She is loving and generous. She is dependable and has great endurance.

Possible characteristics of this person are:
- Nurturer,
- Preserver,
- Traditional,
- Family-oriented,
- Endurance.

THE KING OF PENTACLES

The King of Pentacles card represents a mature male of marriageable age, a provider and an achiever. He is a good manager and watchful of his money without being overly cautious. He is disciplined and resourceful.

The King of Pentacles is concerned with the welfare of the family. He is productive, and works hard to accumulate physical resources for those who are near and dear to him. He is physically powerful.

The King of Pentacles is motivated by the necessity of providing for his family or clan. He can be generous without loss of practicality. He is status-oriented and focused on worldly gain. He is driven to produce, build, and change the physical world.

Possible characteristics of this person are:
- Provider,
- Achiever,
- Generous,
- Practical,
- Determined.

The Suit of Cups

This suit of the Minor Arcana is named Cups in almost every Tarot deck. This may be because cups as containers are as prevalent today as they were when Tarot cards first became common.

The suit of Cups is identified with emotions, with water, and sometimes with other liquids that might be used to fill cups. The cards in this suit are all concerned with emotions, regardless of whether they are expressed (positively or negatively) or repressed. Cups cards deal with emotional matters, relationships, caring, feelings, creative and artistic expression, sentimental activity, and the ebb and flow of all emotional states. Emotions are a necessary and important part of being fully alive, even for individuals who try to suppress them personally and in others.

When Cups are numerous in a layout, it signals the reader that the information in the reading concerns the client's emotions and his or her reactions to experiences and events.

THE ACE OF CUPS

The 1 or Ace of Cups card represents ecstasy, a temporary but delightful feeling of being blessed, of experiencing perfection, of having attained emotional fulfillment. The ecstatic individual feels the full bloom of a peak emotional experience, free from all worry.

The Ace of Cups is a highly desirable card. It can signify a marriage proposal joyfully accepted or the confirmation of a mutually desired pregnancy. More likely, it can mean a breakthrough in emotional communication accompanied by a feeling of exaltation.

The cup of emotions is full. All the pleasant emotions combine into a state of undiluted joy that feels wonderful. The experience is in no way diminished by the knowledge that the condition is only temporary.

Possible meanings are:
- Ecstasy,
- Emotional peak experience,
- Mutually desired marriage proposal accepted,
- Mutually desired pregnancy confirmed,
- Emotional communication breakthrough.

THE 2 OF CUPS

The 2 of Cups card signifies lovers in harmony, in which two are emotionally as one. There is a balance of emotions in the union of opposites who willingly give and take. The flow of emotions is strong and steady in a very natural and non-threatening manner for both.

The 2 of Cups can signify marriage and partnership. For lovers separated by circumstances not of their choosing, it can be a sign of reconciliation. There can be renewed cooperation in relationships, which from an emotional standpoint are extensions of the self.

The individual's reservoir of emotional vitality gives a feeling of being complete, of being able to ride the flow of emotions without sinking into unpleasantness. This card often points to successful love in a harmonious marriage.

Possible meanings are:
- Lovers in harmony,
- Emotional balance,
- Marriage,
- Partnership,
- Reconciliation.

THE 3 OF CUPS

The 3 of Cups card is about the sharing of love. The emotional life is flourishing. Things underway will come to a conclusion that is pleasant for everyone. Love continues to expand and to grow.

The card may indicate the birth of a child that both will love. With emotional decisions correctly made, love continues to unfold in harmony and joy.

Lovers will enjoy the blossoms and fruits of their love. This love can be a bonding force that makes them individually feel part of the group or community. If there has been sickness, the healing has already begun. If comfort is needed, it is now available.

Possible meanings are:
- Love shared,
- Flourishing emotional life,

- Possibility of having a child,
- Healing,
- Comfort.

THE 4 OF CUPS

The 4 of Cups card frequently indicates that certain emotional rewards are available but veiled from awareness. The rewards can be attained if the person realizes that the problems causing wariness of involvement are more imagined than real.

The individual may be suffering from undirected anger that may explode or produce negative affects. The aggression or anger must be transformed into positive energy. This transformation will help the person to regain the path to emotional maturity.

This card indicates that defensiveness is probably excessive, not warranted by the circumstance. This is a time to survey those things that have been overlooked, to release lingering anger that does not pertain to the present situation, and to discard old emotional baggage.

Possible meanings are:
- Unseen but available emotional rewards,
- Imaginary problems,
- Remembered anger,
- Excessive defensiveness,
- Old emotional baggage.

THE 5 OF CUPS

The Five of Cups card indicates disappointment. Something that was wanted is no longer available, and the individual is focused on what has been lost instead of what remains. The result is an emotionally depressed state. The amount of guilt, sadness, shame, and worry is much greater than the amount of loss suffered.

This card indicates a period of emotional confusion. The individual has overanalyzed feelings to the point that he or she cannot appreciate the good things remaining. If depression continues, the person may need help from a close friend or professional counselor in order to regain perspective and halt a downward spiral of frustration and suffering.

The person experiences difficulty in enjoying things without becoming attached to them.

Possible meanings are:
- Depression,
- Anger,
- Frustration,
- Suffering,
- Attachment.

THE 6 OF CUPS

The 6 of Cups card indicates enjoyment of friends, family, and past associations. There is a possibility of a gift or an inheritance coming. Memories bring pleasure and emotional warmth but are not free from the possible specter of sorrow.

Too much nostalgia is hazardous; things are not what they used to be. The danger of looking backward is that the person may stop appreciating the present and become mired in self-pity that reinforces inappropriate emotions.

This card signifies that the individual must be ready to undergo an emotional purification process if sorrowful memories have displaced the enjoyment of the present. Tears for what might have been may be needed to wash away attachments to the past.

Possible meanings are:
- Enjoyment of friends and family,
- Possible gift or inheritance,
- Sorrow from excessive nostalgia,
- Emotional purification,
- Tears.

THE 7 OF CUPS

The 7 of Cups card is a reminder of the danger of fear. Fear must be recognized for what it is. Is it based on reality? Phobias and paranoia planted in the imagination can grow large and overwhelm the individual with illusory problems that have no real existence except in the mind that holds onto them.

Fear can be created by emotional greed, hindering the individual from attainment of emotional goals. The fearful individual becomes withdrawn, secretive, emotionally closed, and inexpressive. This process leaves the individual in a hidden place where the negativity of fear is the dominating influence on life.

All fears can be named. Once they are named, they become less terrible and easier to deal with on the emotional level. This is the time to examine and name fears so that the individual is not fearful of fear itself.

Possible meanings are:
- Fear,
- Emotional greed,
- Paranoia,

• Unwarranted dread,
• A need to name and define fears.

THE 8 OF CUPS

The 8 of Cups card identifies a time of emotional stability based on a degree of maturity created by experience and growth. This is a time for emotional rest before a new phase is begun. The new phase will, in all probability, lead to greater emotional understanding.

This period of emotional stability may be a period of emotional stagnation. Despite the recognized need for greater emotional understanding, a certain fatigue must be overcome before a new drive for emotional satisfaction can be undertaken.

This card signifies a time to emotionally unwind while everything seems to continue in a routine manner. Let the lack of present excitement be a resting place, a time of quiet that may be boring but is necessary before the next emotional wave arrives.

Possible meanings are:
• Emotional stagnation,
• Emotional stability,
• Fatigue,
• Routine events and activities,
• A rest period preceding a new emotional drive.

THE 9 OF CUPS

The 9 of Cups card indicates enjoyment and contentment, a feeling of emotional satisfaction derived from achievements. Beauty graces the person's environment, all the emotional support systems are in place, and the individual is happy with the general conditions of life.

This is the time of fulfillment. Efforts have been rewarded, talents recognized, and material benefits accrued. The person feels in tune with the emotional spirit of the times.

This card signifies an emotional maturity that is itself an outstanding achievement. The pettiness of envy, jealousy, and coveting has been shed like an old garment. The individual is comfortable in the new clothes of positive emotions that bring satisfaction without pain and joy without reservation.

Possible meanings are:
- Enjoyment,
- Contentment,
- Fulfillment,
- Satisfaction without pain,
- Joy without reservation.

THE 10 OF CUPS

The 10 of Cups card signifies passions realized. Life is rich with meaning. Excitement is balanced with awareness. There is no desperation because passion is felt as a daily reality; life is fully enjoyed.

A major emotional cycle has been completed, bringing fulfillment of wishes. Energy—emotional energy—is a great resource and is never exhausted. The ups and downs of competing emotions are a thing of the past. Maturity has harnessed the passion for life so that rich and exciting emotions are always available.

This card indicates satisfaction of the passions without diminishing them. The emotional cups of life are brimming with all that is desired. There is no hurry to drink, because the cups cannot be drained. The thrill of life constantly renews itself.

Possible meanings are:
- Passion,
- Emotional fulfillment,
- Exciting emotional base for life,
- Desires satisfied,
- Emotional maturity achieved.

THE PAGE OF CUPS

The Page of Cups card represents a young person, probably a child who has not yet experienced puberty. This person is emotional, sensitive, and sentimental. This individual spontaneously expresses feelings, no matter how fleeting, in an open, honest, and quite unsophisticated way. Most of the emotions flow swiftly.

The Page of Cups is inclined to be a bit dreamy but is basically good and willing to help others. This individual has courage in situations that call for it. He or she seeks emotional change and is looking for new emotional opportunities and emotional guidelines.

The individual represented by this card is mostly concerned with the emotional side of life in all aspects. He or she needs and wants emotional guides to help shape an increasing awareness of the emotional complexity of life and relationships. This person is also concerned with individual tastes.

Possible characteristics of this person are:
- Below the age of puberty,
- Seeking emotional change,
- Courageous,
- Expressive,
- Wanting emotional guidelines.

THE KNIGHT OF CUPS

The Knight of Cups card represents a young person of either sex who is past the age of puberty but not yet married. This youth is emotional and sensitive, and may be the younger lover of an older partner or possibly the student of an older, learned person.

The Knight of Cups identifies a person who has a nurturing nature, capable of emotional growth and learning. Other probable characteristics are expansiveness, creativity, and loyalty—especially to family and friends.

This person is sensual and tender, proceeding toward emotional maturity at a rapid rate. He or she makes a dedicated and motivated relation, lover, friend, or associate who will honor commitments as well as contribute honest effort to joint projects.

Possible characteristics of this person are:
- Unmarried,
- Emotionally growing,
- Expansive,
- Dedicated,
- Motivated.

THE QUEEN OF CUPS

The Queen of Cups card represents a mature woman of marriageable age. She is extroverted and emotionally outgoing, with an unusual ability to sense the emotions of others. She is creative and enchanting.

She rejoices in the positive emotions of life's events. She is artistic, confident, and involved with her chosen associates. She has a soothing, nurturing nature that others experience as a healing influence.

She is concerned with emotions, her own as well as those of family, friends, neighbors, and associates. She is motivated by a loving nature that strongly influences her behavior. Her strength and many talents are often unsuspected by others.

Possible characteristics of this person are:
- Extroverted,
- Emotionally outgoing,
- Rejoicing,
- Involved,
- Talented.

THE KING OF CUPS

The King of Cups card represents a mature man of marriageable age. He is a leader who volunteers his efforts to help others. He has an affinity for the sea. He is not only dependable but also very resourceful.

The King of Cups is a kind and considerate leader who never shirks from his responsibilities. He expresses his emotions, showing compassion and mercy for those that he leads.

He has strong persuasive powers, but knows the value of compromise—not only with others but with his own inclinations. He guards against a slight tendency toward personal laziness, self-indulgence, and the enjoyment of decadence. He calculatingly discriminates which emotions to express, and enjoys the exhilaration of emotional highs.

Possible characteristics of this person are:
- Leader,
- Volunteer,
- Persuasive,
- Calculating,
- Enjoys emotional highs.

The Suit of Swords

This suit of the Minor Arcana is traditionally called Swords in almost all Tarot decks. Some modern decks use other names to avoid the idea of weapons associated with destruction.

The suit of Swords is identified with the mind and all mental activity. The cards in this suit are all concerned with the workings of the mind—the creative tool of humanity that defines individual reality based on input and insights. The mind is the seat of consciousness. Intelligence is the mind's cutting edge, which slices perceived reality into shapes and sizes that can be used for present understanding as well as remembered for future use. Swords deal with thoughts, ideas, decisions, memory, learning, and all the other actions and qualities associated with mental activity.

When Swords are numerous in a layout, it signals the reader that the information in the reading concerns the client's mind and the client's mental activity.

THE ACE OF SWORDS

The 1 or Ace of Swords card represents new insights, new concepts, and new ideas. The mind now acts with brilliance that can be likened to an awakening. Shadows and confusion dissolve in a flash of light that brings great clarity to all matters at hand.

The Ace of Swords signifies excellent communication within the mind itself and with other minds. There is a new and important understanding of the sources and processes of belief systems, philosophies, moral structures, and ethical standards. Willful ignorance is abolished as the mind becomes aware of its powers. These powers, including analysis, logic, and rational thinking, become apparent at this time. The individual should use them to the fullest extent and develop an appreciation for them.

Possible meanings are:
- Sudden insight,
- Clarity of thinking,
- Intellectual understanding,
- An end to confusion,
- Increased mental powers.

THE 2 OF SWORDS

The 2 of Swords card indicates the ability to see both sides of a present issue and hold possibly conflicting choices while determining where the balance is located. It signifies an end to one-dimensional thinking, an awareness of duality that the mind must evaluate.

The 2 of Swords can symbolize two alternative answers to a question. The mind is not swayed by arguments designed to appeal to the emotions only; it recognizes that emotions form no basis for rational discussion.

This card symbolizes the vast spectrum of possibilities that exist between two extremes and suggests that the best two be combined into a rational compromise.

Possible meanings are:
- Mental balance,
- Seeing both sides,
- Recognition of emotional arguments,
- Seeing more than one possibility,
- Making wise compromises.

THE 3 OF SWORDS

The 3 of Swords card symbolizes the triangle, a strong support for any structure. It suggests the strength and expanse of the mind that is capable of seeing a middle ground beyond the illusion of duality.

This card represents a stage of mental growth in which all things are not seen as black or white but as multiple shades of gray. The power of the mind reveals a spectrum of ideas that is wide and deep instead of a narrow band defined by two extremes.

There is a threefold blossoming of the mind that allows the individual to consider wider choices, broader horizons, and participate in areas of mental activity that were not previously perceived. The mind becomes a strong support system that allows the individual to make mental excursions into what was unknown or neglected territory.

Possible meanings are:
- Strength of mind,
- Seeing beyond the illusion of duality,
- Mental growth,

- Wider mental choices,
- Interesting mental excursions.

THE 4 OF SWORDS

The 4 of Swords card is concerned with the use of logic, one of the mind's most powerful tools. Using logic, the individual can chart a course that is understandable, possible, and open to unexpected changes that can be managed.

This is a time to reflect on the logical means of making future choices, to weigh the actions of the past and decide if they should be continued. Thus the mind can be used as a laboratory of experience and a factory of ideas that will more likely produce the desired results. This is a time for creating new mental foundations based on logic. Speculative actions should cease.

Possible meanings are:
- Logical thinking,
- Charting a new course,
- New plans,
- New mental foundations,
- No speculative ventures.

THE 5 OF SWORDS

The 5 of Swords card indicates a flurry of mental activity after a period of relatively calm reflection. There may be some mental confusion due to the sheer number of things to be considered. Activity at this time is mental rather than physical; plans and decisions should be made before any action is taken.

It is not a time to consider things leisurely because there are numerous details to be resolved. Solutions to problems must be found rapidly. Attend to getting things into the proper order despite other distracting considerations.

This card indicates a need for rapid but thorough thinking in order to avoid confusion and carelessness that could lead to future problems. Now is the time for speeding up mental processes to find correct answers within the limited time available.

Possible meanings are:
> • Flurry of mental activity,
> • Confusion,
> • No time for leisurely thinking,
> • Many problems to be solved mentally,
> • Mental speed required.

THE 6 OF SWORDS

The 6 of Swords card indicates the need to apply the mind to appropriate tasks. A great deal of progress is now possible through proper mental effort. New ideas will be welcomed if the thinking needed to promote them is done skillfully.

This is the time of accepting responsibility, of rendering mental service where it is required. There is a strong chance of a higher attainment through mental effort. There is a great deal of energy available for productive use.

There is emotional support in this card for the mental actions required. Publicity is favorable if it is ethically generated. New projects can be well thought out at this time, with a good chance of successful completion.

Possible meanings are:
> • Mental application to proper tasks,
> • Progress,

- Promotion,
- Good publicity,
- Emotional support of mental effort.

THE 7 OF SWORDS

The 7 of Swords card indicates that good advice and counsel are going to be offered. Mental plans that have been well thought out can now be turned into physical action. Good ideas should be written down so that they can be shown in solid form to those concerned.

This is a time of action based on previous mental efforts. Trusted friends can be consulted. Associates will be receptive to well-planned projects that show depth of mental effort. Advanced education of either a formal or informal nature can be successfully undertaken now.

The necessary mental preparations have been made. There is no reason for further delay. Projects can be begun on time and finished according to schedule. No hesitation is required or desirable when opinions are called for.

Possible meanings are:
- Good advice offered,
- Physical action,
- Write down ideas,
- Further education,
- Voicing of opinions.

THE 8 OF SWORDS

The 8 of Swords card indicates that the combining of ideas from diverse sources is now taking place. New understandings can be achieved as connections are made among ideas that were previously separated in the mind. A synthesis of many things learned long ago will bring new insights and greater comprehension.

There can be a blending of mind, body, and spirit that creates a bond between mental ideas, spiritual experiences, and emotional realizations. There is an almost overwhelming grasp of what an integrated mental system can accomplish. Philosophy is comprehended not in the abstract but as a tool to shape reality, foster action, and achieve a higher level of integrated mental activity than was previously thought possible. The excitement of mental activity has reached a peak that was previously hidden in the clouds.

Possible meanings are:
- Combining of ideas,
- New insights,
- Greater understanding,
- Integrated mental activity,
- Mental excitement.

THE 9 OF SWORDS

The 9 of Swords card indicates that major decisions must be made, some of which will be difficult. Unpleasantness is associated with the problems confronting the mind. There may be disappointment regarding deception that may come from within or be due to outside forces. If associated cards in the layout suggest ill health or sudden changes, this card may indicate the possibility of death.

This card also signifies a narrowness of mind that can be either negative or positive. In the negative sense, the individual suffers from self-imposed mental restrictions such as a limited point of view, willful ignorance, or logic-tight compartments in the mind. In the positive sense, the individual can sharply and narrowly focus on what problems actually exist and turn away from idle speculations, wishful thinking, and unlikely scenarios.

Possible meanings are:
- Difficult decisions,
- Unpleasantness,
- Deception,
- Death,
- Restriction or focus of mind.

THE 10 OF SWORDS

The 10 of Swords card is the card of delusion. These are delusions of the mind, created by the desire to see what is not there, to interpret reality in ways that are not justified by the data. These delusions are self-created products of mental distraction.

This is the time for major philosophical change, for purging the mind of outmoded thoughts and impractical and self-deluding beliefs. This must be done so that the individual can grow. The operative delusional systems are childish habits that block the path to maturity and wholeness.

These delusions damage the self and others; they must be abandoned. More attention should be paid to intuitive input and the meaningful feedback that comes both from one's environment and from others.

Possible meanings are:
- Delusion,
- Erroneous thought,
- Damaging beliefs,

- New philosophy needed,
- Pay attention to intuition.

THE PAGE OF SWORDS

The Page of Swords card represents a child of either sex who may be on the threshold of puberty. This person represented is somewhat secretive and investigates people and events in a manner designed to be undetectable. This individual is mentally alert, very curious, and has a great desire to learn in an independent manner.

The Page of Swords is thoughtful and vigilant, with a certain grace of movement that helps him or her appear unobtrusive while observing everything. The observation is not noted by others because the child appears to pay attention to something else. This individual is hungry for intellectual stimulation and knowledge, especially regarding those things that adults tend to conceal or not explain.

Possible characteristics of this person are:
- Approaching puberty rapidly,
- Secretive,
- Curious,
- Great desire to learn,
- Seeks restricted information.

THE KNIGHT OF SWORDS

The Knight of Swords card represents a person of either sex who is past puberty but has not yet contemplated marriage. This youth has a surprising amount of knowledge, which is attributable to a thirst for information, and an aggressive, sometimes rash, approach to obtaining experience of the world.

The person identified with this card has great respect for formal education and is inclined to be a perfectionist. He or she is a great defender of systems of ideas, regardless of whether tested or not. Such dogmatic beliefs and actions are often a handicap in dealing with others who distrust ideas that are inherently imprudent.

Possible characteristics of this person are:
- Youthful,
- Knowledgeable,
- Rash,
- Aggressive,
- Defender of untested belief systems.

THE QUEEN OF SWORDS

The Queen of Swords card depicts a full-grown woman who may or not be married but has mothering attributes. Although protective of herself and others, she is strong-minded and assertive. She is secure in her extensive knowledge of herself and the world. The Queen of Swords is willing to fight for what she knows is right and understands what tactics are effective in hostile encounters.

She likes fresh air and has little toleration for stuffy situations, narrow-minded people, and small-minded ideas. She puts her personal idealism to practical use in her dealings with the world. Her skills as a researcher, teacher, or mentor are formidable. Her philosophical and studious nature does not deter her from being aggressive when that is effective or practical.

Possible characteristics of this person are:
- Mothering instincts,
- Willing to confront,

- Idealistic,
- Skilled teacher,
- Studious and philosophical.

THE KING OF SWORDS

The King of Swords card is a mature male who may or may not be married. He is mentally creative, capable of generating new and useful ideas, and is conversant with science and technology. He is a defender and protector who may have military or quasi-military experience.

The King of Swords is a clear thinker, capable of making wise decisions in a firm manner. His alertness enables him to accumulate knowledge that others seldom tap. His extensive experience has been analyzed, filed away in his mind, and is available for appropriate use as needed. He is motivated by necessity and understands the use of tactics in difficult situations. He is willing to use revolutionary approaches if necessary.

Possible characteristics of this person are:
- Creative,
- Defender and protector,
- Clear thinker,
- Extensive experience,
- Willing to change the world.

7

★

The Suit of Wands

This suit of the Minor Arcana is traditionally called Wands in most Tarot decks. A few decks name this suit Staffs or Rods. Each card in the suit usually depicts the icons as long shafts of wood, sometimes with a budding twig to indicate its living energy.

The suit of Wands is identified with spirituality and energy, the inner fire that burns within each individual. All the cards in this suit are concerned with the spirit and passions of the individual, not necessarily sexual, whose intensity produces the energy that burns like an internal flame. This suit deals with all matters of the spirit, all things in life that make a person feel positively energized. This includes working at occupations or avocations that fulfill an inner need or desire, and express creative energy and deeply felt aspirations.

When Wands are numerous in a layout, it signals the reader that the information in the reading concerns the client's spirit and energy.

THE ACE OF WANDS

The 1 or Ace of Wands card represents a spiritual centering, an illuminating awakening. This can be a sudden great insight or may have been preceded by a period of conscious spiritual work or a search for personally valid answers.

The Ace of Wands signifies something new and fortunate, such as creative insights, good luck, an unexpected gift or inheritance, a rebirth, or possibly an addition to the family through birth or legal proceedings. This new thing is very positive, which assures the completion of important goals. A new understanding of the forces of internal energy enables the individual to achieve objectives with deep inner meanings. This could be a breakthrough in the person's occupation, possibly the transformation of an avocation into a desirable occupation or enjoyable sideline.

Possible meanings are:
- Spiritual centering,
- Spiritual awakening,
- Unleashing of positive energy,
- New understanding,
- Positive changes in occupation.

THE 2 OF WANDS

The 2 of Wands card indicates a spiritual choice to be made, with intuition playing the most important role in making the choice. Alternatives with great potential must be selected on the basis of a pure spirit. Great adventures are being offered but they must be viewed with discrimination.

The 2 of Wands can symbolize twin spiritual paths

that each beckon with the possibility of growth and excitement. The perception required to make the proper choice involves more than logic; the spiritual needs and aspirations must also be considered. A holistic approach is required in order to embrace all the spirit and energy of the individual concerned.

The potential for experiencing wondrous events and activities is strong. Only the spiritually aware choice is the correct one.

Possible meanings are:
- Spiritual choices,
- Intuition is important,
- Alternatives available,
- Adventure possible,
- Holistic approach.

THE 3 OF WANDS

The 3 of Wands card represents a combining of energetic forces, possibly in a business or occupational venture that can be approached with optimism and confidence. If a partnership is formed, it should be with others of a strong and practical nature.

This card signifies a time to be open to opportunities, with compassion for all who may be involved. New events may be associated with a visionary insight. Major achievements are a distinct possibility through the proper use of existing power as well as combined wisdom.

There is an end to adversity. Profits and rewards await the individual who responds with the vision of improving things for all concerned. Energy is available to achieve goals that are productive and satisfying.

Possible meanings are:
- Combining of energetic forces,
- New business or occupational venture,
- Optimism and confidence,
- Practical partners,
- Visionary insight.

THE 4 OF WANDS

The 4 of Wands card indicates that spiritual centering has occurred. The individual has found harmony and is comfortable on the path of spiritual growth and development. This is a card of peace and of balance. There is support, perhaps from a sponsor, for spiritual growth.

The 4 of Wands suggests a celebration to recognize achievements. There may be a holiday feeling as the individual reviews his or her blessings. Life feels right and secure.

No difficult striving is currently required. The person's honesty is recognized and rewarded. Energy flows in a steady stream to keep everything on the correct course.

Possible meanings are:
- Spiritual centering,
- Harmony,
- Celebration,
- Honesty recognized,
- Good energy.

THE 5 OF WANDS

The 5 of Wands card indicates that there is work to be done, and courage is needed. After passing through a period of stability, the individual is again facing uncertainty. There is still freedom of choice, but the choices are numerous, complicated, and confusing. Each choice has the possibility of reward, but first the path must be cleared with intensive effort.

The 5 of Swords indicates a time to review priorities, to think things through and make new plans. Existing belief systems must be examined because they will be challenged by the confusion of choices. Only the person involved can determine if these belief systems are valid in this situation. If they fail to provide useful answers, then they must be changed, replaced, or abandoned to create the spiritual constructs that will yield the answers required.

Possible meanings are:
- Difficult work,
- Uncertainty,
- Courage required,
- Review priorities,
- Examine belief systems.

THE 6 OF WANDS

The 6 of Wands card depicts victory after a difficult contest. There is recognition of spiritual values gained and appreciation for the energies expended. Progress has been made without moral compromise. The trust placed in others has been rewarded and shown to be justified.

The 6 of Wands shows that the period of waiting is over, and that longed-for results are materializing. The individual can relax and appreciate what has been accomplished. Rewards and promotions are to be bestowed on the individual who exemplifies how to harness spiritual energy, without injuring others. These good examples will be seen as something from which others can learn. The person involved is appreciated by others as a teacher who personally shows the way.

Possible meanings are:
- • Victory,
- • Recognition,
- • Reward,
- • Promotion,
- • Appreciation.

THE 7 OF WANDS

The 7 of Wands card shows the individual having to face tough competition. Inner energy is needed to light a darkened field. A refinement of one's belief systems may be required if events in the near future are to have the desired results. These events are physical but their impact will affect spiritual values.

The 7 of Wands indicates that negotiations will be successful. Indecision may handicap necessary compromises. Strength and courage will help the individual triumph over delays and difficulties. Relationships will greatly improve as problems are overcome by ethical means. Advice offered, especially unasked-for advice, should be carefully heeded. Although victory is virtually assured, it will not come without work.

Possible meanings are:
- • Tough competition,
- • Adjustment of beliefs,
- • Strength and courage required,
- • Improved relationships,
- • Probable victory.

THE 8 OF WANDS

The 8 of Wands card indicates that harmony is being achieved via the middle path. Emotional forces and spiritual energy are balanced in a way that provides peace of mind. There is a confirmed sense of purpose. Energy is at a high level.

The path of spiritual growth is firmly established. Rapid advances may come soon. The condition of harmony through balance is not accidental, but the result of cutting away the undergrowth of distractions so that the path is obvious. The individual's sense of purpose leads to a situation of great promise and happiness. Disputes and quarrels can be settled in an ethical manner. Differences are resolved by honorable and open means.

Possible meanings are:
- Harmony,
- Emotions and spirit working together,
- Confirmed sense of purpose,
- High energy,
- Disputes settled ethically.

THE 9 OF WANDS

The 9 of Wands card indicates that the individual must be true to his or her values and retain integrity in the face of challenges. Any difficulties now are similar to past difficulties that have been overcome. This time, unexpected or hidden resources are available to aid the individual whose mental and spiritual energies are united.

The 9 of Wands signifies that losses suffered in conflict are minor in nature. The individual should focus on the larger view, which gives promise that the adverse circumstances will be overcome.

It is a time for integrating the spirit and the mind to help oneself deal with the vagaries of life. From this comes strength in reserve, the sources of which cannot be lost.

Possible meanings are:
- Integrity retained,
- Difficulties are minor,
- Unexpected resource,
- Integration of spirit and mind,
- Strength in reserve.

THE 10 OF WANDS

The 10 of Wands card indicates spiritual growth and the completion of a long cycle. But it is not the end, because spiritual growth can spiral upward throughout life if the individual is willing to work with the paradoxes involved. A certain spiritual fulfillment has been attained, but not the end of the journey for the person who desires to experience the ultimate in spiritual growth.

There may be a certain hesitation, a time for pausing to recharge for the next level of attainment. Presently there is excellent spiritual communication. The person should consider exploring beyond the experiences sought by the average seeker. These areas, although complex, hold a promise that is now only suspected—the promise of mastering the realm of the spirit.

Possible meanings are:
- Spiritual growth,
- A long cycle completed,
- Spiritual attainment,
- A time for pausing,
- Spiritual mastery possible.

THE PAGE OF WANDS

The Page of Wands depicts a child of either sex who has not yet reached puberty. This child has bountiful energy and seeks information about the spiritual aspects of the world. The child wants to learn about intuition, insight, and inspiration in order to satisfy an inquisitive and sensitive nature that may be quite introspective.

The Page of Wands is concerned with transmission of information and may act as a go-between or messenger. Sometimes the messages are delivered in person but frequently the telephone or post system is used to cover the distances involved. This energetic person is interested in communicating the news to all concerned, especially when pertaining to new opportunities, unexpected events, and exciting ideas. This person seeks spiritual growth and expansion.

Possible characteristics of this person are:
- Near puberty,
- Inquisitive,
- Sensitive,
- Introspective,
- A messenger.

THE KNIGHT OF WANDS

The Knight of Wands card represents a young person of either sex who has not yet married. This person tends to be impetuous, delving deeply into events and situations, trying to get to the bottom of things that others might prefer left alone.

The person identified with this card is often interested in metaphysics and religion as they pertain to spiritual knowledge and development. He or she is impatient with the slow pace and regimentation of formal society, which sometimes hampers the development of this person's natural brilliance. This person is a leader with high energy, but requires inspiration to act. The Knight of Wands carries messages from which he is always learning, even though he does not always understand their contents.

Possible characteristics of this person are:
- Youthful,
- Impetuousness,
- One who stirs things up,
- Impatience with formality,
- Messenger and student.

THE QUEEN OF WANDS

The Queen of Wands card depicts a woman who has attained her majority. She is vibrant and bright, expert in metaphysics and other matters pertaining to the human spirit. She may be a channel for insight into the unknown. She is sensitive and sensuous, capable of passionately giving and receiving love.

Her charm enables her to moves swiftly and gracefully through obstacles that might stymie others. Her formidable knowledge of the world is primarily experiential, obtained by watching and seeing how others accomplish things. She is skilled at adapting means to assure worthy ends. Her aggressiveness, although never hostile, may be unexpected by others and can arouse resentment when discovered. Her wisdom sometimes makes others think she is all-knowing, although she knows better.

Possible characteristics of this person are:
- Vibrant,
- Bright,

- Knowledgeable in metaphysics,
- Sensuous,
- Wise.

THE KING OF WANDS

The King of Wands card depicts a mature male who may or may not be married. Easily fulfilling the role of spiritual advisor, he is both intuitive and introspective. He is skilled in the ways of mediation. His introspection sometimes causes him to delay in reaching an opinion, but his judgments are characterized by justice. He has the potential to be an effective healer through the use of his hands.

The King of Wands has a spiritual and passionate nature. He understands a variety of belief systems to which he has been exposed in his lifetime. His bearing is that of a minister, and he may have considered becoming one. He keenly understands the force of necessity in his own life and in the lives of others. He is secure in his own identity to the extent that he feels no need to defend who he is. This enables him to act out the various roles that are appropriate to his position in life.

Possible characteristics of this person are:
- Spiritual advisor,
- Intuitive,
- Introspective,
- Mediator,
- Secure in his identity.

8

Learning the Layouts

Once you have learned the meanings of the cards, the hardest part is done. You should be pleased with having accomplished the most time-consuming step in becoming a reader. The next thing you must learn is one or more layouts, which refers to particular ways of dealing the Tarot cards so they can be interpreted for a client. There are innumerable possible layouts you can use, or you may even invent your own. Learning any specific layout is relatively simple. All you have to do is select a layout from this book or from any other source. Next, learn its two basic elements. The first element of any layout is the sequence of its card positions. The second element is the meaning or significance of these positions. After this, the most important thing about any layout is to have a clear idea what each position means at the time of the reading. Therefore, each card should be dealt in a logical and reasonable sequence, with each position distinctive enough so that it will not be confused with any other.

Different texts understandably recommend different layouts. This is because authors describe the layouts that they personally find to be effective, revealing, and useful. Each author may have developed these layouts over years of experience. They may come from traditional sources, or they may be adapted from a nontraditional source favored by the author.

Depending on the kind of information they are designed to reveal, the pattern and number of cards used in individual layouts vary enormously. In all cases, however, the reader uses the meaning of each position and the meaning of each card to obtain the basic information given to the client. There is nothing sacred about any layout. There is nothing in the layout that you as the reader cannot change on a temporary or permanent basis if that improves the quality of the reading. But do not change any layout until you are completely familiar with its original form. You should select one layout to learn on the basis of your own personal preference. The next five chapters each describe a separate layout. Experiment with several layouts to learn which one seems most comfortable or easy for you to use. Use that layout as your main vehicle.

Another aspect of any layout is whether it is aesthetically pleasing to view and use. Tarot cards are colorful to see, and reading is interesting work. The layout should form a pattern that is distinctive and visually comprehensible to both client and reader.

Typically, in any layout all cards are dealt face-up and the reader waits until all the cards in the layout are dealt before interpreting them for the client. This enables the reader to get an overview of the cards as they are dealt. Another method is to deal the cards face-down, turning them up one at a time for individual interpretation before going on to the next. After they have all been turned face-up and individually discussed, the reader provides an overview of the cards.

The overview gives the reader important information about the broad aspects or framework of the overall reading. How many Major Arcana cards are in the layout? These represent important aspects of the client's life. How many cards from each Minor Arcana suit? These tell the reader how much of the reading is concerned with the physical, emotional, mental, and/or spiritual portions of the client's life. How many court cards? The court cards often tell the reader about other people involved in the client's life. They also may represent characteristics of the client, depending on their positions. Although each card represents some specific portion of the client's life, the proportion and blend of the types of cards seen in the overview also contributes greatly to the overall reading.

Each succeeding chapter about a layout includes a sample reading so that you can gain a perspective on how to communicate the information to the client. The sample readings are only elementary outlines of actual readings. They are intended to sketch the basic dynamics of each layout and to serve as a groundwork to use in developing your own personal and flexible style.

Use each sample reading as a study tool. One effective way to do this is to first separate out the cards that are used in the sample reading. Then arrange them in the order shown and deal them into the positions shown. Carefully examine the cards while studying the sample reading. Consider and try to understand the many elements involved in a Tarot reading. After studying the sample layout and reading for some time, try changing one or more cards in the layout and determine how that would change the reading.

Many readers have a layout that they prefer to use the first time they read for a client. This is generally a layout that gives information about the past, present, and future. If the client becomes a repeat client, the reader may want to use other layouts for subsequent readings. Use ones that place less emphasis on the past and deal more with the client's concerns about the present situation and the near future.

ADDITIONAL LAYOUT INFORMATION

Some clients will be satisfied with the reading as presented by the reader, but others will want additional information about individual cards in the reading. There are various additional abbreviated layouts that can be used to expand on the meaning of any particular card in a primary layout in order to answer these questions. Since any of these additional layouts can be used with any of the primary layouts described in the subsequent chapters, they are separately described here.

THE EXPANSION LAYOUT

The Expansion Layout merely consists of dealing more cards from the deck around the card about which more information is wanted. This card is called the key card.

Layout Positions:
1 4
KEY
2 3

Significance of the Positions:
[1] Origin,
[2] Motivation,
[3] Effect,
[4] Outcome.

As the reader interprets the cards in positions 1 through 4 pertaining to the key card, the additional meanings revealed should be related to the specific information gained in the previous primary reading. Other key cards may be selected from the primary reading for additional Expansion Layouts. The reader may also modify or alter the Expansion Layout in any way that is useful or meaningful.

CHANGES LAYOUT
Another method of gaining more information about a particular card in the primary reading is the Changes Layout. To do this layout, deal four cards from the top of the deck next to the key card. Deal them face-up in a row after the key card.

Layout Positions:
KEY 1 2 3 4

Significance of the Positions:
[1] Effect of the key card on the client,
[2] Change in the client's environment,
[3] Near-future changes in the client's outlook,
[4] Eventual or distant-future changes in the client's outlook.

As in all methods of gaining additional information about a primary reading, the reader relates and integrates this additional information into the overall reading.

NEAR-FUTURE LAYOUT

This layout provides a quick look at the near future. It can be appended to any reading or can be used as a short, separate reading of its own. Deal four cards from the deck in any convenient place.

Layout Positions:
1 2 3 4

Significance of the Positions:
[1] The coming event,
[2] Internal response of the client to the event,
[3] The action the client will take,
[4] The significance (of the event, the response, and the action).

YES OR NO LAYOUT

If the client has a question, the reader can use five cards from the deck to give the client a Yes, No, or Maybe answer—even if the reader does not know what the question is. The reader may have no idea whether the client is looking for a Yes or a No.

Deal five cards from the deck in a straight line or row.

Layout Positions:
1 2 3 4 5

Significance of the Positions:
All positions have equal value. A majority of positive meanings indicates a probable Yes. A majority of negative meanings indicates a probable No. The lack of a clear majority of negative or positive meanings signifies Maybe.

The Flower of Life Layout

Deal the cards from the deck in the sequence shown by the following numbers. Position the cards so that their corners touch as shown, creating a representation of a blossoming flower.

Layout Positions:
```
  2  5  8
1  4  7  10
  3  6  9
```

This layout is called the Flower of Life because it depicts an organic process that takes into account the various factors in the client's life that contribute to the flowering or answer to the client's query.

Significance of the Positions:
[1] Past,

[2] Client,
[3] Foundation,
[4] Environment,
[5] Present,
[6] Energy,
[7] Focus,
[8] Expectations,
[9] Results,
[10] Future.

SAMPLE FLOWER OF LIFE READING

The Cards in the Sample Layout:
[1] 5 of Pentacles,
[2] Knight of Swords,
[3] Ace of Pentacles,
[4] Page of Swords, Reversed,
[5] 7 of Wands, Reversed,
[6] 11—Strength, Reversed,
[7] 10 of Cups, Reversed,
[8] 8—Justice,
[9] 6—The Lovers, Reversed,
[10] 7—The Chariot, Reversed.

SAMPLE FLOWER OF LIFE INTERPRETATION

The reader points to the first card, in *position 1*, and says, "The position of this card refers to something in the *past*. Here the card dealt is the 5 of Pentacles. The suit of Pentacles deals with tangible things, things that can be seen and touched. What this card in this position tells me is that in the past you have suffered a serious difficulty that pertains to the physical world. This could have been a financial problem, a health problem, or the failure of a project that you expected to be successful."

At this point the reader pauses briefly to accept any feedback that the client may wish to give—anything from a nod of agreement to providing the details of the difficulty. Denial is unlikely since almost everyone has had some difficulty in the past. If the client gives specific feedback such as saying that he or she broke a leg in an automobile accident, the reader should carefully weigh its influence during the rest of the reading. If the client provides no feedback, accept this as the client's choice and go on.

The reader points to the next card, in *position 2*, and says, "The position of this card represents you, the *client*. Here is the Knight of Swords. It indicates that you are knowledgeable and pursue experience aggressively, sometimes leading you to do things that others might consider rash."

The reader pauses for feedback. As before, the reader accepts and weighs the importance of any feedback.

The reader points to the next card, in *position 3*, and says, "The position of this card represents your *foundation*, the kind of support you have. Here is the Ace of Pentacles, a card about things that are tangible. It represents the reality that other people can see. It signifies success and abundance. It indicates that you have enjoyed more than average success in the physical world as a foundation for your life. It could also mean good health throughout most of your life."

The reader pauses for feedback.

The reader points to the next card, in *position 4*, and says, "This card is in the position that pertains to your *environment*. Here is the Page of Swords. It is reversed, facing you instead of me. The card ordinarily represents a curious child, but when reversed means that the curiosity is diminished or blocked in the circumstances. Or you may have a childlike eagerness to learn information that is not readily available. It could also simply mean that there is a curious child in your life."

The reader pauses for feedback. Whatever the client mentions here will be valuable feedback for the reader.

The reader points to the next card, in *position 5*, and says, "This card is in the position that represents *present conditions* in your life. Here is the 7 of Wands, reversed. The suit of Wands is concerned with your spirit, your motivation, the inner forces that cause you to act. This card indicates that you will need strength and courage to develop relationships that you want. Present events may affect your belief systems—the way that you view the world."

The reader pauses for feedback.

The reader points to the next card, in *position 6*, and says, "The position of this card represents the *energy* you have involved in the present situation. Here is Major Arcanum 11—Strength. The Major Arcana is like a suit of trumps, so this card is especially important. It indicates that you must have fortitude and courage to develop the relationships you want. Because the card is reversed, the strength you need to deal with present events is hampered in some way."

The reader pauses for feedback.

The reader points to the next card, in *position 7*, and says, "This card is in the position that tells about your *focus* on your current situation. Here is the 10 of Cups, reversed. Cups is the suit that deals with emotions, and this card indicates that you are strongly emotionally involved. You have a passionate interest in the outcome of events. The reversal of the card may mean that it won't be easy to satisfy all of your desires."

The reader pauses for feedback.

The reader points to the next card, in *position 8*, and says, "This card is in the position that defines your *expectations*. This is what you expect and hope for, but not necessarily what you will get. Here the card is Major Arcanum 8—Justice. It means that you expect balance and harmony."

The reader pauses for feedback.

The reader points to the next card, in *position 9*, and says, "This card is in the position that tells about *results*. The previous card was about what you expect. This card identifies what you are likely to get, what the results will be. Here the card is Major Arcanum 6—The Lovers, reversed. This card means the union of opposites. It indicates that you will get the harmony you want, possibly in a successful romance. The reversal means that the path will probably not be smooth, but the results indicate a correct choice."

The reader pauses for feedback.

The reader points to the final card, in *position 10*, and says, "This card is in the position about your *future*. Here is Major Arcanum 7—The Chariot, reversed. It symbolizes movement and indicates that you have the energy to pursue your goals. Reversed it means that the path to your goals may be impeded, so that some extra push will probably be necessary for you to get what you want. But it is attainable.

"Altogether, it appears probable that you are going to get what you want from the present situation. There are some twists and bends in the road that you'll have to deal with, but you definitely seem to be on the right road. It looks probable that you will succeed in the matter."

At this point, the main thrust of the reading is complete. The reader now asks the client if there are any questions about the reading or if more information is desired about any of the cards in the reading. If so, the reader can do an Expansion Layout with that card as the key card. (Refer to the previous chapter.)

In closing, the reader lets the client know that the reading represents only what the reader has seen as possibilities. The reader adds that no guarantee comes with the information. It is up to the client to determine what use, if any, to make from it.

The Clock Layout

Deal the cards in the sequence indicated by the numbers below. Position them so that the empty space in the center of the layout is about equal to the size of four cards. Side-by-side cards touch each other.

Layout Positions:

```
     12   1
10   11      2   3
 9    8      5   4
      7   6
```

Significance of the Positions:

[1, 2, and 3]   Early influences,
[4, 5, and 6]   Present situation,
[7, 8, and 9]   Near future,
[10 and 11]   More distant future,
[12]   Completion of cycle and new beginning.

This layout is called the Clock because it deals with events in the client's life in relation to time. When using this layout, the reader should try to ascertain how the cards relate to time. If the client wants information within a certain time frame of months or years, that gives the reader a good idea of the time scale involved. If no time scale is suggested, the reader may assume that the cards start with the client's early life and proceed to the completion of the current cycle.

SAMPLE CLOCK READING

The Cards in the Sample Layout:
[1] 7 of Cups, reversed,
[2] 13—Death,
[3] 7 of Wands, reversed,
[4] 4 of Cups,
[5] 20—Judgment, reversed,
[6] 4—The Emperor, reversed,
[7] 0—The Fool,
[8] 2 of Swords,
[9] Page of Swords,
[10] 19—The Sun, reversed,
[11] 15—The Devil,
[12] King of Wands.

SAMPLE CLOCK INTERPRETATION

The reader points to the first three cards dealt in the layout, in *positions 1, 2, and 3*, and says, "The positions of the first three cards all represent *early influences*."

The reader now points to or touches the first card and says, "Here the first card is the 7 of Cups, reversed. The suit of Cups represents emotions. This card indicates that one of the major emotions you experienced, either early in your life or early in your involvement with your present concerns, was fear. Because the card is reversed, it means that the fear was not as severe as it might have been. But it was there, and it was real to you."

If the client makes no comment, the reader points to the next card, in position 2, and says, "This card is Major Arcanum 13—Death. The Major Arcana always deals with something more important than everyday occurrences. The card named Death signifies a sudden, unexpected change of great magnitude. It very rarely means the death of a person. In this case it probably means that your early fear came to a sudden, complete end."

The reader pauses for feedback.

The reader points to the next card, in position 3, and says, "This card is the 7 of Wands, reversed. The suit of Wands represents spirituality and motivating forces. We are still dealing with early influences. This card indicates that when the fear ended, it was replaced with enough strength and courage to get you through the early situation and into the present one. I hope that this information about early influences is meaningful to you."

Although this is not a question, the reader pauses to allow for feedback that will provide information about the reading so far. If there is feedback, the reader listens to it carefully and then continues.

The reader now points to the next three cards, in *positions 4, 5, and 6*, and says, "These three cards all represent your *present situation*. Here the first of these cards is the 4 of Cups, which is in the suit dealing with emotions. It means anger. Currently you feel anger that you can turn into positive energy. The next card is Major Arcanum 20—Judgment, reversed. It seems to signify that your anger comes from an opinion or decision made about you, probably by someone else but possibly your own judgment of yourself. The last card in this set dealing with your present situation is Major Arcanum 4—The Emperor, reversed. This card is about authority, decisiveness, and organizational ability. It means that if you can forgive or understand that judgment, it will lead to greater decisiveness and achievement through your organizational ability. If it were upright instead of reversed, it would mean that you had already understood or forgiven the judgment involved."

After pausing for feedback, the reader continues by pointing to the next three cards, in *positions 7, 8, and 9.* "The positions of all three of these cards represent the *near future*, the things that could start happening today, tomorrow, or next week. Here the first of these cards is also the first card of the Major Arcana: 0—The Fool. It symbolizes the beginning of a journey. It indicates that you are now ready to start what seems like a new journey of great possibilities. The next card here is the 2 of Swords. The suit of Swords deals with mental activity. This card indicates that during this journey or experience, your way of thinking will enable you to see both sides of the issues. You retain your emotional balance, recognizing emotional arguments for what they are. The last card in the set, in position 9, is the Page of Swords. It often represents an alert child who is eager to learn. It may be a child in your environment or it could represent your own eagerness to learn what you need to know to complete this cycle of life."

After allowing for feedback, the reader points to the next set of two cards, in *positions 10 and 11.* "The positions of both of these two cards represent your more *distant future*, the things that will happen during your journey. Here the first card of this set is Major Arcanum 19—The Sun, reversed. Even reversed, it is a very positive card that indicates you will find harmony in life and ultimately realize your goals. The other card here in this set is Major Arcanum 15—The Devil, which symbolizes ignorance and prejudice. This is probably related to the previous card about learning and indicates why The Sun was reversed. It means that you will learn to overcome any prejudice that impedes the achievement of your goals. Literally, the sun shines on you and helps your projects succeed."

After pausing for feedback, the reader looks at the final card in the layout, in *position 12*, and says, "The position of this card identifies the *completion of a cycle* and a new beginning. It represents the completion of one journey and the beginning of another. Here the card is the King of Wands. Wands are the cards of the spirit. The King of Wands indicates that in the completion of this cycle you will become the person represented here, a person who is spiritually mature, very intuitive, and capable of dealing with whatever comes next."

The reader has now told the client the basic information that the cards in their positions have revealed. The reader summarizes the reading by saying that the cards indicate that the client will be going on a journey, perhaps a journey of discovery. During this journey the client will learn what is necessary to achieve his or her goals. This will require the client to overcome some degree of ignorance and prejudice. Greater maturity and capability will be the rewards at the end of the journey.

If the client has a question about one or more of the cards, the reader can continue the reading by using one or more of the additional expansion layouts described in Chapter 8. The reader may also find other useful and meaningful methods of expanding the reading.

In closing, the reader lets the client know that the reading represents only what the reader has seen as possibilities. The reader adds that no guarantee comes with the information. It is up to the client to determine what use, if any, to make from it.

The Triangle Layout

Deal the cards in the sequence indicated by the numbers below. Position the cards next to each other.

Layout Positions:

```
11  12  13  14  15
   7  8  9  10
     4  5  6
      2  3
       1
```

Significance of the Positions:

[1] The client's current situation,

[2 and 3] Next factors in the pattern of events,

[4, 5, and 6] Effects of 2 and 3 on the client's life,

[7, 8, 9, and 10] Next changes to come,

[11, 12, 13, 14, and 15] New factors stemming from the emerging pattern.

If time and the reader allow, the client can select the card for position 1 from either the entire deck or just from the Major Arcana (with all the cards face-up and open to view). Tell the client to pick a card that he or she thinks pertains to the present situation. If time is limited or if you prefer not to let the client examine all the cards, shuffle them as usual and let the client pick one without looking at the faces. Or simply let the client cut the cards. If the client is allowed to pick from face-up cards, the deck should be shuffled seven times and the remainder of the positions dealt as usual.

The advantage of letting the client pick the card for position 1 is that the client will frequently offer personal information to the reader afterwards. This is especially true if the client asks the reader what the selected card means. When the reader tells the client its meaning, the client's acceptance or refusal of the card indicates the client's present situation or concern. This feedback provides the reader with a framework for the reading.

The disadvantage of this procedure is that the client may have difficulty deciding, taking more of the reader's time.

SAMPLE TRIANGLE READING

The Cards in the Layout:
[1] King of Swords,
[2] 10 of Pentacles, reversed,
[3] 4—The Emperor,
[4] 12—The Hanged Man, reversed,
[5] 4 of Pentacles, reversed,
[6] 18—The Moon, reversed,
[7] 2 of Wands,
[8] 9—The Hermit, reversed,

[9] 21—The World, reversed,

[10] 9 of Cups,

[11] 6 of Swords,

[12] King of Pentacles, reversed,

[13] 3 of Swords,

[14] 5 of Wands, reversed,

[15] 3 of Pentacles.

SAMPLE TRIANGLE INTERPRETATION

During the reading, the reader allows for feedback from the client with brief pauses as appropriate. The reader should encourage feedback but not require it, as some clients may be unwilling.

To begin, the reader points to the first card, in *position 1*, and says, "This card position represents you as the *client* in your present situation. Here is the King of Swords. The suit of Swords deals with mental activity. This card indicates that you are a creative and experienced person who thinks clearly and is willing to make changes in the world."

The reader points to the next two cards in the layout, in *positions 2 and 3*, and says, "The positions of these next two cards represent the *next factors in the pattern* of events in your life. The first of these two cards is the 10 of Pentacles, reversed. The suit of Pentacles deals with tangible things, the physical aspects of the world. This card indicates that you will receive material rewards for your efforts. Because the card is reversed, it signifies that the rewards may not be as great as possible. However, they will not be miserly."

After pausing for any feedback, the reader continues: "The other card in this set is Major Arcanum 4—The Emperor. Since it is from the suit that is like a trump suit, it is especially important. This card identifies an authority figure who is organized and decisive. It could represent the position you will hold. It might represent someone that you work for, perhaps someone who is going to provide some of the rewards that you will receive and that are expected because of the previous card."

After pausing for any feedback, the reader points to the next row of cards, in *positions 4, 5, and 6*, and says, "All three of the card positions in this row identify the *effects* in your life of the last two cards, namely the reward and the authority figure.

"Here the first card in this row is Major Arcanum 12—The Hanged Man, which represents a situation that is slow to change. The situation is not unpleasant but seems static. This card indicates there will not be much change for awhile after you receive the rewards. The card is reversed, which probably indicates that the static period will not last long."

The reader points to the next card, in position 5, and says, "This is the second effect of the new factors. Here the card is the 4 of Pentacles, which indicates that you will start a new endeavor. The suit of Pentacles pertains to the physical world. This card is reversed, which may indicate some initial problems with the new endeavor that will, however, be successfully overcome."

The reader points to last card in the row, in position 6, and says, "This is the third effect of the new factors. Here the card is Major Arcanum 18—The Moon, reversed. It indicates a cycle of gradual change and evolvement. Because the card is reversed, it means that you may be impatient with the slow process of the cycle."

The reader pauses for any feedback and makes comments in response. The reader then points to the next row of cards, in *positions 7 through 10*, and says, "All the positions in this row of cards are identified with the *next sequence of changes*.

The first of these changes is represented by the card in position 7, which is the 2 of Wands. The suit of Wands deals with motivational forces and spiritual aspects of the individual. This card indicates that a spiritual choice must be made. You need to pay attention to your intuition as well as your logic in considering your spiritual aspirations."

The reader points to the next card, in position 8, and says, "This card is Major Arcanum 9—The Hermit, reversed. It suggests a time of partial withdrawal from the affairs of the world in order to develop spiritually and come to a philosophical understanding of your life. Because it is reversed, it means the withdrawal will be limited in time and scope."

The reader points to the next card, in position 9, and says, "This card is Major Arcanum 21—The World, reversed. It indicates that you will emerge from The Hermit period knowing that you are in the center of things, feeling whole and successful. The fact that the card is reversed may mean that you may need some time to adjust to this new knowledge, but it shouldn't be a problem for you."

The reader points to the last card in the row, in position 10, and says, "This card is the 9 of Cups. The suit of Cups deals with emotions. This Cups card indicates that you will experience fulfillment and contentment as a result of these changes."

The reader, after pausing for feedback, goes on to point to the cards in the final row, in *positions 11 through 15*. "The positions of the last five cards in the layout define the *new factors* in your life that complete the pattern started by the first card. The first of these cards, in position 11, is the 6 of Swords. The suit of Swords deals with aspects of mental activity. Here the 6 of Swords indicates progress and promotion through mental effort."

The reader points to the next card in the last row, in position 12, and says, "This card is the King of Pentacles and represents a person with whom you will be associated. This person is a manager type who is practical, generous, and determined."

The reader points to the center card in the last row, in position 13, and says, "This card is the 3 of Swords, which means mental growth and wider mental choices."

The reader points to the next card, in position 14, and says, "Here the card is the 5 of Wands, reversed. The suit of Wands deals with motivation and spirit. This card indicates that you should review your priorities to eliminate uncertainty. The card is reversed, which means that the task will not be easy but it can be accomplished."

The reader points to the last card in the layout, in position 15, and says, "The final card is the 3 of Pentacles. It deals with the physical world. The card signifies that the outcome of this entire pattern is a high level of productivity leading to material gains and monetary rewards."

After pausing for feedback, the reader summarizes the reading. "Your pattern here is one of growth and material gain. None of the cards indicate any problems that will overtax your abilities. All you have to do is pay attention to what is going on and make the best decisions you can. The majority of the cards indicate that you will be rewarded for your efforts. The rewards are not only physically tangible, but will also be experienced as mental and spiritual growth, as well as emotional satisfaction."

The reader has now told the client what the individual cards mean and has summarized the client's pattern of experience by saying that the client's future looks especially promising. The reader should now respond to any questions about the reading or about the meaning of any particular card. If the client wants more information about one or more cards, the additional layouts described in Chapter 8 can be used. The reader also reminds the client that the information presented in the reading cannot be guaranteed, for it represents only a possible future whose outcome is up to the client alone.

The Pyramid Layout

Deal the cards in the sequence indicated by the numbers below. The first 15 cards all touch their adjacent cards. Cards 16 and 17 stand alone as shown.

Layout Positions:
```
                  15
               13   14
        16   10 11 12   17
             6  7  8  9
          1   2   3   4   5
```

Significance of the Positions:

[1, 2, 3, 4, and 5] People and events in the client's life,

[6, 7, 8, and 9] Factors that connect the people and events,

[10, 11, and 12] How the client presents reality
    to others,
[13 and 14] How the client presents reality to self,
[15] Meaning of the pattern when completed,
[16] Describes the pattern as it waxes or develops,
[17] Describes the pattern as it wanes or completes.

SAMPLE PYRAMID READING

The Cards in the Layout:
[1] King of Wands, reversed,
[2] Queen of Wands,
[3] 10 of Cups,
[4] 9 of Pentacles,
[5] 2 of Cups, reversed,
[6] 3—The Empress, reversed,
[7] 9—The Hermit,
[8] 8—Justice, reversed,
[9] 20—Judgment, reversed,
[10] 4 of Pentacles,
[11] Page of Pentacles,
[12] 8 of Pentacles, reversed,
[13] King of Cups,
[14] 3 of Pentacles, reversed,
[15] 21—The World,
[16] 3 of Swords, reversed,
[17] Ace of Pentacles.

SAMPLE PYRAMID INTERPRETATION

In the following, as in all readings, the reader pauses as
appropriate for possible feedback from the client. To begin, the
reader looks over the cards and says, "There are a number of

Major Arcana, which are the cards that could be considered trumps—and that means some very significant things are happening. Also, there are more cards from the suit of Pentacles than from any other suit. Since Pentacles deals with the physical world, things that can be seen and touched, this reading will deal with the tangible things of the world."

The reader points to the bottom row of cards, in *positions 1 through 5*, and says, "All the card positions in this row represent the *people and events* in your life. The first card, in position 1, is the King of Wands, reversed. This card represents a person in your life, a man who is a mediator, perhaps a spiritual advisor. He will usually give you useful and intuitive advice. But because the card is reversed, his advice may not always be helpful."

The reader points to the next card, in position 2, and says, "This is the Queen of Wands. This card represents a woman who is sensitive and bright. She is also spiritually knowledgeable. Since she is positioned next to the man represented by the first card, they probably know each other. They may be married. They could represent your parents."

The reader points to the next card, in position 3, and says, "This is the 10 of Cups. The suit of Cups deals with emotions. This card signifies that you have some emotional maturity and that you are passionately involved with the things that are happening in your life."

The reader points to the next card, in position 4, and says, "This card is the 9 of Pentacles, a card pertaining to the physical world. It indicates that you have had material success in the world and enjoy your life, probably with more leisure now than during most of your life."

The reader points to the last card in the first row, in position 5. "This card is the 2 of Cups, reversed, and deals with emotion. It indicates some sort of partnership that needs tuning to provide the emotional balance you want."

The reader pauses to give the client an opportunity to comment on what has been said. Going on, the reader then looks at the next row of cards, in *positions 6 through 9*, and says, "All the card positions in this second row identify *factors that connect people and events* in your life. In this reading, the fact that they are all Major Arcana cards is unusual and very significant, indicating that these factors are centrally important. The first card, in position 6, is Major Arcanum 3—The Empress, reversed. This card represents a female authority figure who knows the man and woman represented by the first two cards in the reading. She might be a grandmother. The reversal of the card indicates that she possibly tends to be possessive and sometimes shallow from your perspective."

The reader points to the next card, in position 7, and says, "This is Major Arcanum 9—The Hermit. This card indicates that you have reached your present position after some period of introspection and re-evaluation that gave you much greater understanding and wisdom."

The reader points to the next card, in position 8, and says, "This card is Major Arcanum 8—Justice, reversed. This card means that you are taking responsibility for your actions and decisions, and in that way avoiding guilt. The card is reversed, which may indicate that you reached this position because of impersonal forces that made irresponsibility an option that was not open to you."

The reader points to the last card in the second row, in position 9: "This card is Major Arcanum 20—Judgment, reversed. It suggests forgiveness, and could refer to the partnership indicated by the card in position 5. You may have to forgive both that partner and yourself to feel all the emotional freedom that you want."

The reader now points to the third row of cards, in *positions 10, 11, and 12.* "All the card positions in this third row are about *presenting your reality to others*, the reality of the things revealed by the cards so far. The first card in this row, in position 10, is the 4 of Pentacles. It means that, by your actions, you are showing other people that you are making a new beginning, and that you feel confident about it."

The reader points to the next card, in position 11, and says, "The Page of Pentacles indicates that you recognize you have some learning to do. You don't hide this fact. In some respects, you feel like a child and seek to change or grow up by gaining more knowledge."

The reader points to the next card, in position 12, and says, "The 8 of Pentacles, reversed, means that you communicate to others that you believe in yourself and possess everything you need to successfully complete your projects. If it was upright instead of reversed, you would probably be telling people that most of your projects are already completed."

The reader now points to the two cards in the next row, in *positions 13 and 14.* "The two card positions in this row are both about *presenting reality to yourself*, about how you see this reality in your own mind. The first card, in position 13, is the King of Cups. It indicates that you see yourself in control of the situation, that you understand your own spirit and motivation."

The reader points to the other card in this row, in position 14, and says, "This card is the 3 of Pentacles, reversed. It indicates that you feel certain of realizing the growth and rewards that you are seeking. If it was upright instead of reversed, it would probably mean that you already see yourself as having most of the growth and reward you want."

The reader now points to the card that tops the pyramid, in position 15, and says, "The card position at the top of the pyramid refers to the *meaning of the completed pattern* to you. Here the card is Major Arcanum 21—The World, which couldn't be better in that position. It means that your actions and ideas are right. You should get all the things you want."

The reader now points to the card at the left of the pyramid, in *position 16*. "This card position denotes the *characteristics of the pattern as it develops*. The card here is the 3 of Swords, reversed. This card indicates that you will experience mental growth as the pattern takes form. Because the card is reversed, this growth will probably require a considerable amount of mental effort."

The reader now points to the card at the right of the pyramid, in *position 17*. "This card position is about the *completion of the pattern*. Here it is the Ace of Pentacles, which strongly indicates tangible success in the world."

At this point, the reader pauses to receive any feedback from the client. After this, the reader summarizes the reading. "Altogether, this is an extremely positive reading. No serious problems seem to be coming your way. All you have to do is pay attention to what is going on, do what you think is the best, and you will get everything you want."

The reader has now told the client what the cards have revealed in this reading. Given this very encouraging reading, the client may be completely satisfied and have no further questions. If the client does ask questions, the reader should answer them as completely and honestly as possible. An additional layout, such as one described in Chapter 8, can also provide more information about any of the cards. Before concluding, the reader should explain that the reading has revealed only possibilities, and that nothing in it should be considered a certainty.

13

The Octave Path Layout

Deal the cards in the sequence indicated by the numbers below. The cards all touch adjacent cards.

Layout Positions:
1 2 3 4 5 6 7 8
9 10 11 12 13 14 15 16
17 18 19 20 21 22 23 24

Significance of the Positions:
[1] Past views,
[2] Past intentions,
[3] Past speech (action),
[4] Past conduct (action),
[5] Past vocation (action),
[6] Past effort (action),
[7] Past alertness (action),

[8] Past concentration,
[9] Present views,
[10] Present intentions,
[11] Present speech (action),
[12] Present conduct (action),
[13] Present vocation (action),
[14] Present effort (action),
[15] Present alertness (action),
[16] Present concentration,
[17] Future views,
[18] Future intentions,
[19] Future speech (action),
[20] Future conduct (action),
[21] Future vocation (action),
[22] Future effort (action),
[23] Future alertness (action),
[24] Future concentration.

In this layout, the eight cards in each of the three rows are a feedback system that reports on the client's experience of life in the past, present, and future, respectively.

SAMPLE OCTAVE PATH READING

The Cards in the Layout:
[1] 7 of Wands,
[2] 2—The High Priestess, reversed,
[3] 4 of Swords,
[4] Knight of Cups,
[5] 21—The World, reversed,
[6] 5 of Cups,
[7] 6 of Wands,

[8] 18—The Moon, reversed,
[9] 0—The Fool,
[10] 15—The Devil, reversed,
[11] Page of Pentacles, reversed,
[12] 9 of Swords,
[13] Queen of Pentacles,
[14] 8 of Pentacles,
[15] 10 of Swords, reversed,
[16] 6 of Swords,
[17] 6—The Lovers,
[18] 10 of Wands,
[19] 2 of Wands, reversed,
[20] 2 of Swords, reversed,
[21] 8 of Swords, reversed,
[22] 10—Fortune, reversed,
[23] 1—The Magician, reversed,
[24] 8 of Wands.

SAMPLE OCTAVE PATH INTERPRETATION

During the reading, the reader pauses as appropriate to receive any feedback from the client. Any information from the client may make the reading more meaningful. The reader should be certain to inform the client that any feedback is welcome, because the client may believe that he or she should not say anything to interrupt the reader's narrative flow.

To begin, the reader points to the first card in the top row, in *position 1*, and says, "This card position is about your *past views*, how you saw the world and how you saw yourself. Here it is the 7 of Wands. The suit of Wands deals with spirit and motivational forces within the individual. This card indicates your awareness of the strength and courage required to deal with the tough competition you faced in the past."

The reader points to the next card in the first row, in *position 2*, and says, "This card position concerns your *past intentions* as based on your views. Here the card is from the Major Arcana, the suit of the most important cards which are like trumps. This card, Major Arcanum 2—The High Priestess, reversed, indicates that your past intention was to expand your consciousness and become wise. The reversal of the card may mean that your intentions were not completely fulfilled in the past."

The reader points again to the top row, to *positions 3 through 7*, and says, "The next five card positions all deal with your *past actions*. There is a card position each for speech [3], conduct [4], vocation [5], effort [6], and alertness [7]."

The reader points to the third card in the first row, in *position 3*. "This card position is concerned with your past *speech*. Here is the 4 of Swords, which signifies that your past speech was based on your logical thinking. All cards in the suit of Swords are concerned with thinking and all other mental activity."

The reader points to the next card, in *position 4*, and says, "This card position deals with your *past conduct*. Here is the Knight of Cups. It identifies a person whose conduct was honorable, based on motivation and dedication. The card describes your conduct in the past."

The reader points to the next card, in *position 5*, and says, "This card position symbolizes your *past vocation*. The card is Major Arcanum 21—The World, reversed. This card expresses your feeling of having had almost unlimited choices of occupation and your confidence that you would do well. Because the card is reversed, your choices were more limited than you thought."

The reader points to the next card, in *position 6*, and says, "This card position is about your *past effort*. Here is the 5 of Cups. The suit of Cups deals with emotional aspects of life. This card indicates a disappointment, some frustration and suffering over the results of your work. You felt that your efforts didn't produce the results you wanted or that some of your work was not appreciated at that time."

The reader points to the next card, in *position 7*, and says, "This card position is about your *past alertness*. Here it is the 6 of Wands, from the suit that deals with the spirit and personal motivational forces. The card suggests that being alert about how you were expending your efforts brought you more of the appreciation and reward you wanted."

The reader points to the last card in the first row, in *position 8*, and says, "This card position is about your *past concentration*. It's about how you focused on your actions to see what you could learn from them. It is Major Arcanum 18—The Moon, reversed. This card symbolizes a phase of mental growth that you experienced as a result of past concentration. The reversal of this card indicates your impatience for this phase to begin or that you had some trouble incorporating the intuitive part of this growth into your concept of how you act and react in the world."

The reader looks over the cards in the second row and says, "The second row of cards deals with the same subjects as the first row except this row represents the present."

The reader now looks over the cards in the middle row and says, "This second row of cards deals with the same subjects as the first row, except that it represents the present instead of the past."

The reader points to the first card in the middle row, in *position 9*, and says, "This card position is about your *present views*. It is Major Arcanum 0—The Fool, and it represents a person starting on a journey. It is an excellent card in this position because it signifies that your concentration, represented by the previous card, was effective. Concentration was necessary for you to modify your views based on what you learned from your past experiences. This modification made you feel as if you were starting on a new journey as you turned your past experience into wisdom. This card means that you made the best possible use of your experience."

The reader points to the next card, in *position 10*, and says, "The next card position is about your *present intentions*. Also from the Major Arcana, it is 15—The Devil, reversed. The Devil symbolizes the evils of dishonesty, prejudice, and bigotry. With the card reversed, it indicates your intention to keep these evils out of your life. In other words, your present intentions are extremely positive."

The reader now points to the next five cards in the middle row, in *positions 11 through 15*, and says, "These next five card positions all pertain to your *present action*. We have already established your good intentions, because you updated and changed your views based on previous experience. The cards have also revealed that your intentions match the positiveness of your views. Now we are going to see what the cards can tell us about your actions in the present time. The big question is whether or not your actions will reflect your intentions."

The reader points to the card in *position 11* and says, "This card position is about your *speech in the present*. Here the card is the Page of Pentacles, reversed. This card identifies a person who seeks change. The card is probably reversed to show that it is not a child but a more mature person. That person is you, and it indicates that you seek change in how you express yourself. You endeavor to make your works match your views and intentions. "

The reader points to the next card, in *position 12*, and says, "This card position is about your *present conduct*. Here is the 9 of Swords. The suit of Swords deals with mental activity. This particular card indicates that you have some difficult decisions to make at the present time. It also suggests that you need to take a wider view of things in order to remove any limitations you have placed on your thinking. It is possible that you have not examined all the available alternatives in regard to your decisions."

The reader points to the next card, in *position 13*, and says, "This card position pertains to your *present vocation*. Here is the Queen of Pentacles. It could represent a person involved in your work activities. This is a traditional person, inclined to nurturing and preserving things as they are. If there is no such person in your present work situation, then the card probably pertains to you. It may indicate that you should appreciate and protect your ability in a traditional manner or occupation, because that will prove important to you."

The reader points to the next card, in *position 14,* and says, "This card position represents your *present effort*. Here is the 8 of Pentacles, from the suit that pertains to physical things—things that can be seen and touched. This card signifies that your efforts are worthwhile and are being appreciated in a tangible way."

The reader points to the next card, in *position 15*, and says, "This card position represents your *present alertness*. Here is the 10 of Swords, reversed. It is from the suit that deals with mental activity. This card indicates that you should pay more attention to your intuition. Some of your present thoughts and beliefs have been influenced by delusion and need to be re-examined. It appears that you believe some things that just aren't true. If the card was upright instead of reversed, the situation would be even more serious. In that case, the situation would require you to give this reappraisal your undivided attention."

The reader points to the last card in the middle row, in *position 16*, and says, "This card is in the position of *present concentration*. It indicates what you are learning from concentrating on your actions as shown by the last five cards. It tells that you are learning not only from your actions but from the results of those actions. It answers the question of what are you doing with your input from the real world. Here the card is the 6 of Swords, from the suit that deals with mental activity. This card shows that you are thinking about what you are learning from your actions. You are applying your mental powers to the proper tasks and making progress. It also means that you are already working on getting rid of the delusions that I talked about earlier. This is a very good card for you in this position."

The reader now points to the bottom row of eight cards and says, "This last row, the bottom row, is about the same subjects as the other two rows. But the cards in the last row pertain to the future. The cards in the middle row were about the present. Those cards revealed that you are now concentrating on what your actions have produced and what kind of feedback you have been getting from reality. Now we are going to look into the future and see what the last eight cards can tell us."

The reader now points to the first card in the bottom row, in *position 17*, and says, "This card position is about your *future views*. It is Major Arcanum 6—The Lovers. It symbolizes the union of opposites, which means that you will experience emotional expansion. You will make correct choices that lead to greater harmony than you have previously known."

The reader points to the next card, in *position 18*, and says, "This card position is about your *intentions in the future*. Here the card is the 10 of Wands. All cards in the suit of Wands deal with your inner spirit and motivations—the forces that make you the person you are in terms of aspirations. This card shows that you will complete a long cycle of spiritual growth. It is a very positive indication, suggesting a degree of spiritual mastery that not everyone can achieve in this life."

The reader now points to the the last five cards in the bottom row, in *positions 19 through 24*: "As in the previous rows, the remaining five cards in the row are about your actions. These particular card positions are about your *actions in the future*. The previous two cards about the future have said that correct choices will lead you to views of greater harmony. Your intentions will be directed to spiritual mastery. Now, these last five cards will tell us about your future actions, and whether they are compatible with these views and intentions."

The reader points to the next card, in *position 19*, and says, "This card position identifies your *future speech*. Here is the 2 of Wands, reversed. It indicates that you will become aware of the available alternatives and that you will need to make choices based on your spiritual aspirations. Because the card is reversed, it means that you need to be in touch with your inner drives and your intuitive abilities in order to make these choices properly."

The reader points to the next card, in *position 20*, and says, "This card position characterizes your *conduct in the future*. Here is the 2 of Swords, reversed. It symbolizes your need to see both sides of issues, to recognize emotional arguments for what they are, and to make wise compromises. Again, the reversal of the card means that you need to devote extra attention to your future conduct to make certain that it matches your intentions."

The reader points to the next card, in *position 21*, and says, "This card position deals with your *vocation in the future*. Here is the 8 of Swords, reversed. Since Swords are about mental activity, this card indicates that your work will be mentally exciting. It will be based based on insights, understanding, and combined ideas. reversed, it means that paying attention is particularly important in your work."

The reader points to the next card, in *position 22*, and says, "This card position symbolizes your *efforts in the future*. It is Major Arcanum 10—Fortune, reversed. Its reversal indicates that the fortune you receive for your efforts will not be everything you might imagine. But because the card is from the Major Arcana and is therefore of major importance, even reversed it means that the rewards for your efforts will be considerable."

The reader points to the next card, in *position 23*, and says, "This card position pertains to your *future alertness*. It is Major Arcanum 1—The Magician, reversed. It means trickery and deceit. However, reversed in this position, it signifies that these tendencies to trickery and deceit will be exposed by your alertness to implement your opportunities."

The reader points to the last card in the layout, in *position 24*, and says, "This card position tells about your *concentration in the future*, about how you will focus on the meaning of your experience and your actions. Here the card is the 8 of Wands. Wands are cards of the spirit. This one indicates a new harmony in which your emotions and your spirit work together."

This completes the extensive information that this layout gives about the past, present, and future. The reader should now answer the client's questions and provide any additional information available, as time permits. If the client wants to know more about the delusions that were indicated by the reversed 10 of Swords card in position 15, the reader could use an expansion layout, such as one described in Chapter 8.

In closing, the reader lets the client know that the reading represents only what the reader has seen as possibilities. No guarantee should come with the information. It is up to the client to determine what use, if any, to make from it.

14

About Practice Readings

Having now become familiar with a number of layouts as well as meanings of the cards, the next step is practice readings. These should probably first be done without a client and with reference materials on card meanings and layout positions at hand.

Start by shuffling the deck seven times to remove any existing pattern in the deck. Cut the cards and deal them out in the selected layout. Once the practice layout is before you, begin by looking at the cards to determine what general aspects the cards reveal.

Begin by counting the number of Major Arcana cards in the layout, because they are more powerful than the others. Each Major Arcana card signifies something of special importance in the reading. A high percentage of Major Arcana cards in the layout means the events and circumstances of the client's life are of great significance.

Then look at how many cards there are in each suit of the Minor Arcana to get an overall idea of which areas of life the reading will encompass. The numbered Pentacles cards pertain to the physical world, to things that can be seen and touched. The numbered Cups cards deal with the emotions involved. The numbered Swords cards deal with mental activity such as thinking, perceiving, reasoning, and believing. The numbered Wands cards are concerned with matters of the spirit, of aspirations and motivational forces that guide human behavior and beliefs. The face cards usually represent other people who appear in the reading in relation to the client or aspects of the client's own personality.

Your task as the reader is to tell a coherent story primarily based on the meanings of the cards and the significance of the positions. Each card in a position is an element of the story, shaped by the meaning of the card and the significance of its position in the layout. Consider them as separate scenes in a drama or a motion picture in which the client is at least the protagonist, if not the star. You as the reader are the writer-director who provides the meaning of the scenes and the continuity that weaves them into a dramatic story. Like any other creative endeavor, this can be a difficult task. But reading becomes easier and begins to flow with practice. Eventually an experienced reader will be able to read any combination of cards in a layout as easily as if he or she were reading from cue cards. However, the sensitive reader is always ready to instantly revise the script to incorporate the unique and unpredictable story elements contributed by real people in real situations.

Knowing the meanings of the cards and the positions in the layout enable the reader to create a reading. But as your understanding of the card meanings and the significance of positions grows deeper, your mind will become more free to develop even more entertaining and meaningful readings.

You should speak out loud during the practice reading if at all possible, to an imaginary client if necessary. This will prevent you from skipping over the meaning of any card and from assuming that you could be fluent about any portion of the reading if it were not just a practice reading. Tape recording or videotaping the reading will help you detect any difficulties during your delivery of the information in the reading. As you listen to the tape afterwards, you should be able to visualize the layout and the positioning of each card. If you failed to provide this information, the reading will sound incomplete because all the information that the client deserves has not been adequately presented.

During any practice reading, you may find that the meanings of certain cards seem vague. Look up and study the meanings in other texts and reference materials. Then memorize them. The same is true if you have any difficulty remembering the significance of any position in the layout.

After a practice reading, you should imagine what else the client might ask. Then you provide the answers to the imagined questions. Do this on tape also. This is an opportunity for you to use and practice an expansion layout or other techniques with the cards that provide additional information.

No amount of practice can anticipate the scope and variety of questions that the client might ask about a particular reading. Some clients will not ask anything at all. Others may be insatiably interested in everything about the reading. Some of the general questions that a reader might expect to hear repeatedly from clients and potential clients are posed in Chapter 16, along with possible answers that you might give them. The examples given may or may not be typical of the questions your clients will ask.

Bear in mind that a reading can be somewhat different, or even very different, if the client gives you feedback or significant personal input. Given feedback, you can be more specific about some aspects of the reading. Otherwise you may have to rely on general statements, such as saying that there is someone in the client's life whose situation is worrying the client. If the client then says that she is worried about her mother's health, you've learned part of the specific information that the client is seeking. You can study the cards more pointedly in light of this information.

There is no reason for you to conceal any information from the client concerning how a reading is developed. Giving the client frank answers to all questions is the best way to build the rapport that makes the reading experience better for both reader and client. Do answer any and all questions with as much honesty as you can summon.

Practice readings can be of vital assistance in developing your ability to create a coherent story that represents major aspects of the client's life. The client should find the tale interesting because the client is the subject. Clients are usually interested and involved in their own lives. Most will make a sincere mental effort to connect what you say to the circumstances of their own lives. Clients who identify the information that you present with specific events and causes in their lives are much more apt to be satisfied with the reading and derive the maximum benefit from it, even if the benefit is limited only to entertainment.

You should answer all the client's questions to the best of your ability. Listen to the client's question carefully and then examine the cards already in the layout to see if one or more cards might lead you to an answer. Sometimes relationships among the cards become more apparent after the reading has been summarized for the client. You can obtain a clearer view of what all the cards in the layout combine to reveal.

Your client might ask a question that may not be related to the information in the reading. You should avoid the temptation to seem all-knowing and able to answer everything. This may lead the client to ask any number of questions about things entirely removed from the scope of the reading. You can deal with this situation by telling the client that there is time for only one more question. If the client reacts adversely, advise the client that further questions will only detract from the reading while providing the client with no new information.

Once you feel that you have enough experience by going through a number of complete practice readings, then actual readings can be performed. Usually these first readings will be for other beginning readers or for relatives, friends, and acquaintances. These experiences will help develop your style, brush up your presentation, and confirm that you are ready and qualified to give Tarot readings in a polished manner in exchange for a fee.

As a new reader, you must develop an individual style for dealing with clients. Two major factors in style are honesty and equality. The reader has an implicit obligation to be honest with each client. Honesty means never having to remember a false frame of reference, leaving yourself free to deal with the reality as you experienced it. Equality means treating all clients as if they are equally valuable, entitled to your best possible effort in the reading, and regarded with politeness and respect.

One of the common difficulties that you will experience

is the occasional client who is contemptuous of Tarot readings and Tarot readers. You should view this as an opportunity to show grace under pressure. The main characteristic of a skeptically hostile client is a closed mind, combined with a self-limiting belief system based on very little understanding. Such a person refuses to recognize phenomena that have not been approved by him- or herself or other authority figures. This type of client does not recognize that each individual exists in a separate reality created by the individual's experience as interpreted by the individual's mind. People like this believe that their reality is either the only one or is superior to other's reality. They falsely consider themselves arbitrators of reality when all they are really doing is defending a fragile ego.

Do not argue with such clients and make no attempt to change their minds. Thus you can avoid a useless debate. Acknowledge that the client has a reality that is as useful to him or her as your reality is useful to you. Close the discussion without entering the client's emotionally charged world where nonproductive discussions waste everyone's time.

A minority of clients will become very emotional during a reading. You should be aware of this possibility, which cannot be dealt with in practice. Usually the emotion is associated with something in the client's life that appears in the reading. Accept that the client feels strong emotions but you should not attempt to stop the emotional flow or to join in it. Respect the client's feelings without being swept away by them. If the client's emotions are negative and directed toward you, then you should avoid giving any emotional response that will prolong the emotional display. Remember that the past exists only when you think of it. If the client's emotions are about the past then perhaps you can do or say something that will shift the client's thoughts into the present. The skillful reader will avoid any criticism of the client that may be alienating.

The skilled reader develops a competent, friendly manner. He or she invites the client to relax and appreciate the experience of hearing an entertaining and possibly helpful reading. The client can benefit from a different perspective of events, a wider viewpoint about life, or a clarification of the meaning or significance of his or her actions.

15

★

Clients and Compensation

A beginning Tarot reader's first clients are usually friends, relatives, or acquaintances, and possibly other individuals who are interested in learning to read Tarot cards. These people will have patience with the novice who needs to check source materials during a reading, and whose style and continuity of reading are as yet undeveloped. These clients are a great help to the learning process.

After you reach the point of being relatively independent of source material, you are ready to read for clients at large. By this time you have begun to develop a personal style. You have probably developed a delivery in which your manner and tone is similar to that of a confidant, a trusted friend, or a counselor. Most clients respond positively to a reader who respects and pays attention to them during a relaxed and friendly reading.

Before seeking clients from outside your usual circle, you must decide what sort of compensation you require for giving a reading. Some readers take the barter approach by saying, "I'll give you a Tarot reading in exchange for something of value from you." The thing of value might be a meal, a service, a material object, an exchange of readings, or a sum of money. More frequently, readers specify a particular fee, charge a range of fees on a sliding scale (that is based on the client's financial status), or simply accept whatever the client wishes to donate. Whatever your arrangement, the client should always be aware that your time and effort is valuable.

You should investigate local ordinances before doing any advertising for clients. Some communities, in an effort to protect excessively gullible citizens, either prohibit or place restrictions upon fortune-telling, predicting the future, or forecasting possible future events. Weather forecasters and various other people and businesses are not usually prosecuted under these laws but card readers may be.

If you present card-reading as a form of entertainment, it is unlikely that you will be perceived as someone who is taking advantage of people. However, in some areas, the local authorities may want card readers to obtain an entertainer's license. Usually the civil authorities are only interested in card-reading if it seems to be a business venture or if any local citizens make some sort of complaint.

Calling cards or business cards are a necessity. You should have business-size cards printed with your name and telephone number. The addition of more information is up to you. Listing your address might cause clients to show up at inappropriate times without an appointment or when you are not there. No fees should be mentioned on the card. Whether or not the term "Tarot Readings" or equivalent should appear on the card depends on whether you wish to use the cards for social as well as business use. The most discreet approach is the phrase "Consultations by Appointment." Give the card to each client after their first reading to promote referrals as well as repeat business.

If you decide to advertise, possibly the most productive medium is your local newspaper or shopping news, especially ones delivered free to every street address. Before placing an advertisement, see if there are any similar ads. Investigate to learn what the advertised readers are charging, and whether they consider the ads to be an effective way of finding clients. You might even consider scheduling a reading from a competitor to learn more about their approach and about the process of reading itself.

If you belong to any local organization that publishes a bulletin or newsletter, this is also a possible medium for advertising. A community bulletin board for consumers is another. There are often such boards in grocery stores and laundromats. Any local bulletin or notice board that doesn't charge for display is a potential source of clients. Local organizations with positive interest in psychic or new age matters should be contacted as a possible sources of clients, support, and sympathy. Some religious organizations may be supportive; others, indifferent or hostile.

One of the best ways to attract clients is to arrange to be a card reader at a party or social gathering, where you can do brief readings for a number of people. This could be a fund-raising event for a charity or other worthy cause, a fair of some kind, or even a private party. Whether you receive any financial compensation at one of these functions depends on the circumstances. Sometimes each client pays a small fee for a brief reading. At a private party, the host generally pays a single, larger fee so that the guests are not obligated.

You need a relatively private place to give readings. Since each reading deals with details of the client's life that may be confidential, do not allow spectators except for someone present at the client's request. The private place where readings are given should have a table large enough for the layouts, and chairs for the reader and client. There should be enough light for the reader to see the cards and view the client's expressions and body language. Informal readings in outdoor situations require only a place to sit on the grass or the ground and perhaps a cloth upon which to lay out the cards.

You should time the length of your readings as you give them. It is best to place a clock where it can be seen by you but not the client (to avoid giving the client the feeling of being rushed). Knowing how long each reading generally lasts enables you to schedule readings without keeping clients waiting. How much time to spend answering questions from the client after the primary reading is your decision. When giving multiple readings at a fund-raiser or party, you should make the readings brief if other clients are waiting. The novice reader should schedule individual clients with some leeway between appointments. Even experienced readers like to allow extra time should it be necessary to adequately complete a more complex reading. Not being crowded for time also creates a relaxed atmosphere and better rapport between client and reader.

Some readers like to use various rituals in connection with giving readings. For instance, place one or more small objects on the table, burn incense, or meditate prior to the reading or series of readings. If you give readings in your home, you may want to decorate the room in which readings are given in some way that creates a favorable environment. None of these rituals are essential to becoming a reader, but you may find that they have a positive effect on your readings and your clients. Many entertainers go through a ritual or similar process before a performance to get themselves ready. Readers often do the same.

You must be prepared for feedback from the client. Some clients will treat a reading as an opportunity to reveal their innermost secrets, to describe their deepest problems, or to confess various private actions or thoughts. The client may feel more comfortable giving this information to a stranger than to a friend or professionally trained counselor or therapist. Be prepared to accept this information and help the client deal with these issues within the scope of the reading. Your obligation is to entertain and inform the client, not to sit in judgment. However, you may need to remind some clients that your ability to help them is limited by many factors. Their problems are often not within the scope of a Tarot reading.

16

Probable Questions and Possible Answers

The questions and answers in this chapter are not about any specific Tarot reading. These are probable questions that clients and potential clients might ask about Tarot readings in general or about their own readings. The possible answers are those that might be given by any Tarot reader. As an individual Tarot reader, your own answers will be based on your own personal ideas and experience. You may find find these generalized answers useful as a frame of reference.

WHERE DOES THE
READING INFORMATION COME FROM?

The information comes from what I know about the meaning of the cards and the significance of their positions in the layout. I also use all the knowledge I have from rational and intuitive sources, including what I know about how people think, believe, and behave. I also have some information about the clients, based on how they present themselves insofar as appearance, language, and action. This includes their clothing, mannerisms, attitudes, and body language.

ISN'T THIS DELVING INTO THE OCCULT OR DEVIL'S WORK?

No. What I do is storytelling, a highly respected human activity as old as human language. As a Tarot reader, I speak the words of a story that uses cards instead of pictures, slides, printed words, actors, puppets, film, or tape.

HOW CAN YOU KNOW ABOUT ME UNLESS SOMEONE TOLD YOU?

No one told me anything about you except that you wanted a reading. My experience enables me to interpret the cards and your reactions to them. My information comes from both you and the cards. Some of my readings are more meaningful than others, but I try to make all my readings as meaningful as possible. I have described many things to you in general terms. Some of them may have seemed very specific to you but I have no way of knowing that unless I hear it from you.

WHY DIDN'T THE THINGS YOU SAID PERTAIN TO MY LIFE? THE PERSON YOU TALKED ABOUT ISN'T ANYTHING LIKE ME.

I did my best to give you a good reading. If you think it did not relate to you, that probably means that I am not the person who should read cards for you. I am sincerely sorry that you didn't find it helpful.

WHAT WOULD HAVE HAPPENED IF I PICKED A DIFFERENT CARD TO START?

The information would have been a bit different but very similar overall. Picking a different card would mean that you wanted a different perspective on the information. You would have learned more about one aspect of the reading and less about another. I ask the client to select the first card so that you know you are influencing the cards in the layout. You selected by intuition. So, in a way, you are asking me what would the reading be like if your intuition was different. There are several answers to that. It could mean that you would be a different person than you are and would therefore get a different reading. It could mean that you are interested in other aspects of your life than the ones contained in the reading. There are multiple possibilities for speculation but it wouldn't change anything now because it didn't happen that way. Therefore, you should think about the actual information in the reading and consider how to use it.

WOULD I GET THE SAME INFORMATION FROM ANOTHER READER?

You might get very similar information. I know of many instances in which a client immediately received a second reading from a different reader and reported that it was very similar. It's like hearing the details of a movie from two different people who had similar responses to it. At psychic fairs it is common for a person to get more than one reading and then say that both were similar. Often many of the same cards show up in both readings. But the readings could be different depending on the layouts used, the meanings understood by different readers, and their reader's unique abilities. But speculating on what another reader might tell you is something beyond me. If you are seriously interested, you should consult another reader as soon as possible.

HOW LONG WILL IT BE BEFORE THE THINGS YOU SAID WILL HAPPEN?

It is usually difficult to estimate time in a reading. A lot of the information comes from my intuition, which is not concerned with clock time. In looking at the cards, I make estimates that are both relative and speculative. I can't be sure about the time involved.

DID YOU USE THE CARDS AS A WAY TO GIVE ME ADVICE?

No. If I had seriously just wanted to give you advice, I could have done so without going to the effort required to read the cards. The advice in the reading was based on what I perceived from the cards. I use them to tell a story that relates to your life in some way. I don't make your decisions because you have much more information about your life than I will ever have. If you feel my advice was helpful, I'm pleased. What you do with the information given is up to you.

WHY SHOULD I LISTEN TO WHAT YOU HAVE TO SAY?

Because I am going to tell you an entertaining story about the person you are most interested in—yourself. It will give you the benefit of someone else's perspective on some aspects of your life. Maybe it will help you, or maybe it will be interesting. Only you can decide, but first you have to listen.

MAY I BRING A TAPE RECORDER TO TAPE THE READING?

Yes, I have no objections to that.

I NEVER HAD A READING BEFORE. WHAT DO I DO?

Just listen to what I say about what I perceive from the cards. If you have questions and comments, I am receptive to them. You can speak at any time. After you have received the information, it is up to you to evaluate it. If some of it pertains to possible future events, you cannot evaluate all of it now. So I recommend that you listen and remember it (or tape it if you have brought a recorder). Then you can compare the information to your reality and see if it helps you to understand some aspects of your life.

MAY I BRING A FRIEND WITH ME TO THE READING?

Yes, but you need to decide beforehand whether you want your friend to observe the reading. Since the reading may deal with some private aspects of your life or something that pertains to your relationship with your friend, you might find it embarrassing or awkward.

WHY DIDN'T YOUR READING TELL ME WHAT I WANTED TO KNOW?

If you are willing to tell me what that is, I will deal a few more cards and see what they reveal about it. If you don't want to tell me specifically what that is, rephrase it as a question that can be answered Yes, No, or Maybe. I will deal a few more cards that answer the question. If it cannot be put in the form of a question, I can still deal a few more cards and tell you what they mean in relation to what you want to know.

Sometimes there isn't a good answer to the question as phrased. For example, if your question is "When am I going to buy a new car?" and I don't get any meaningful answer, it might mean that the question is wrong. Maybe you aren't going to buy a new car any time soon for one reason or another, although right now you think you will. Maybe you are going to have an opportunity to buy an excellent used car. Maybe you will have the use of a car in connection with new employment and won't need to buy one. Maybe you are going to get a different car, new or used, through some means that you haven't even considered. Try to phrase your questions without presuming that certain things will happen. Instead of questions based on when, ask questions that can be answered Yes or No. You could ask "Do I need a new car?"

HOW DID YOU LEARN TO DO THIS?

I decided that it was something I wanted to do. So I bought a deck of Tarot cards, and began to learn about the meanings of the cards, the layouts, and giving readings. It took a lot of my time but I thought it would be worth it. From the layouts I studied, I picked one that seemed right for me and memorized it. I began practicing by doing readings without a client, trying to tell an interesting tale based on the cards in the layout. At first I was not very adept but I gradually learned. I have been doing it for some time now and it has gotten easier. Also I think my readings are more entertaining and potentially useful now.

Reading cards is simply an ability that one learns like any other. You improve by doing it. Some people think that it is a talent you are born with, but that's not true. Some people learn it more easily than others, but almost anyone who is motivated to study and memorize can become a Tarot reader.

HOW ACCURATE ARE YOUR READINGS?

Only my clients can judge that. Some of them tell me that my readings are very accurate. Others don't give me any feedback at all. Clients who are regulars—those who return every few months or whenever something new is happening in their lives—come back because they find the readings accurate enough to be useful to them. Some clients don't come back, so I can't verify any predictions I made. I never know why some clients don't come back. Maybe they were satisfied with one reading, or maybe they were dissatisfied and one reading was enough. Friends and acquaintances whom I regularly see tell me that the readings I give them are helpful, but with strangers I only know what they tell me at the time, which may be very little. The clients who return for more readings and recommend me to others usually judge my readings to be more right than wrong.

DO CLIENTS EVER REVEAL EMBARRASSING INFORMATION TO YOU ABOUT THEIR LIVES?

I am able to accept whatever the client tells me without any personal involvement. I accept the information for what it is—something that the client thinks is important for me to know. I treat all information in a reading as confidential. I respect and protect the client's privacy.

DO YOU THINK THAT SOME OF YOUR CLIENTS LIE TO YOU?

It's possible. Sometimes people deceive themselves as a defense mechanism or to feel better about something. Almost everyone occasionally misrepresents themselves, either deliberately or accidentally. Some people believe the lies they tell to themselves. They may present those lies to others as the truth. I give the reading within the framework of doing the best I can with the information and abilities I have. Speculating on whether the client is lying does not help me give a better reading. The client who obviously lies may be deeply overloaded with problems, or perhaps is even trying to invalidate the reading. Either way, I try to concentrate on doing my best.

DO CLIENTS TELL YOU ABOUT THEIR SEX LIVES?
Sometimes, but I don't discuss what they tell me.

WHY DO PEOPLE LISTEN TO WHAT YOU SAY?
Because they want to hear it. If you are lost or confused, you can ask directions from a stranger without placing unlimited trust in the information. A Tarot reading is like that. You don't have to take the information on blind faith. Just listen to it and see if it is useful to you.

DO YOU FEEL RESPONSIBLE IF WHAT YOU TELL A CLIENT CAUSES THEM PROBLEMS?
No. I do take responsibility for the information I give to the client, but I don't present it as immutable truth. The information represents only a possibility that I see. The client decides how to use that information. I take no responsibility for the actions of others, and I never claim that anything in a reading is more than a possibility. It is only my opinion, based on what I discern from the cards. I try to give clients helpful information, but I never tell them how to act.

AREN'T THERE SOME TAROT READERS WHO ARE CONFIDENCE TRICKSTERS?
None that I associate with. There probably have been

Tarot readers who try to bilk clients for additional sums of money, but I don't know any. There are some dishonest people engaged in almost any human activity who will try to take financial advantage of others who seem gullible. But all the Tarot readers I know get paid only for their readings, based on fees agreed to beforehand.

WHY ARE THERE SO MANY DIFFERENT TAROT DECKS?

Tarot cards are like any other commodity. If there is variety, it was created to satisfy the market. All Tarot deck designers have their own ideas about what the cards should be. It takes all kinds of different decks to satisfy different people.

WHAT TYPE OF CLIENT DO YOU FIND DIFFICULT?

Any client who is hostile to Tarot readings in general, or is antagonistic to the reader, is understandably difficult to read for. People who are more interested in their skepticism or unfriendly personal beliefs than acquiring information often block out what is presented. Their negative reactions and statements serve only to destroy any possible rapport with the reader.

DOES THE AGE OF THE CLIENT HAVE AN EFFECT ON THE READING?

Not necessarily. Children or adolescents are often difficult to read for because they are still developing their characters and personalities. Also, they have shorter attention spans, which hampers rapport with the reader.

DO YOU HAVE PSYCHIC ABILITIES?

I don't claim any particular psychic abilities. Tarot reading is not necessarily a psychic process although some clients and readers do hold that belief. I present myself as an entertainer who uses the Tarot cards to tell people possibly informative stories about their lives.

HAVE YOU EVER SAID ANYTHING IN A READING THAT YOU DIDN'T KNOW YOU WERE GOING TO SAY?

Yes, that often happens. Sometimes words come out of my mouth before I'm aware they were in my head. I don't try to block that because I consider it intuitive and spontaneous. There is no way that I can make it happen. I just accept it when it does, in the same way I accept that occasionally I say something unplanned or unexpected in conversation.

CAN YOU DO A READING ABOUT SOMEONE WHO ISN'T PRESENT?

Your question could mean two different things. If you asked me to give you a reading about someone else, the answer would be no. In a reading about you, there might be information about someone else in your life but that is still your reading. If the question means could someone contact me by telephone or mail to get a reading, the answer is that I personally don't do readings that way because I prefer to read for people in person. However, I know that some Tarot readers do readings over the telephone and taped readings by mail.

WHY SHOULD I PAY YOU FOR SOMETHING THAT I'M NOT SURE I BELIEVE IN, WHICH MIGHT NOT BE ANY USE TO ME AT ALL?

If you are already certain that the information I will

give you is worthless, then you shouldn't get a reading from me. In any case, what I am paid for is not the information, but my abilities and my time. My abilities were acquired through study, effort, and discipline; so I expect compensation for their use. My time is also valuable to me; so I expect compensation for its use. I offer a skilled service at what I consider a fair price; you may use it or not, as you choose.

IN MY LAST READING YOU TOLD ME SOMETHING THAT I DIDN'T UNDERSTAND; CAN YOU EXPLAIN IT TO ME NOW?

I give many different readings to different people. Some things stay in my memory but I often do not remember much about any specific reading. I'm willing to give you a reading now if you wish, but I have no meaningful recall of the previous reading. Even if you have a tape recording of it, I am not operating within the framework of that reading now. I would rather see what a new reading would reveal, rather than attempt to explain the previous one to you now.

CAN I TELEPHONE YOU LATER TO ASK YOU MORE ABOUT SOMETHING YOU PREDICTED?

My policy is not to discuss previous readings, even if you want to talk about something that happened as I predicted.

I THINK MY FRIEND NEEDS A READING BUT SHE IS RELUCTANT. HOW CAN I GET HER TO COME FOR A READING?

Your friend has her own reasons for not wanting a reading. I don't try to convince people that they should have a reading.

If your friend is concerned about my fee, you might offer to pay for her reading and see if that removes her objections.

WHAT IS THE RELATIONSHIP BETWEEN RELIGION AND TAROT?

Religion is not connected with Tarot. My religious beliefs are not connected with Tarot readings. There are some religions that encourage the development of such abilities, many that are neutral, and some that are opposed. If I was a member of a religious group that opposed Tarot reading, I wouldn't have spent the time and effort necessary to learn how to do it.

WHERE DID THE USE OF TAROT CARDS START?

There are many different theories about their origin but no proof substantiating any of them. It is known that they became popular in Europe in the Middle Ages, but no clear-cut starting point has ever been established. They may have come to Europe from some Eastern or Middle Eastern area but this is not proven either. Like many other human artifacts, Tarot cards were created at an unknown time by an unknown person or persons. Later they became common. The variety and number of different decks have increased over the centuries as new creators were inspired by existing decks. It is widely accepted that present-day playing cards are adapted from the Minor Arcana. The present-day Joker card is a representation of the The Fool card in the Major Arcana.

IF ALL THE CARDS HAVE DEFINITE MEANINGS TO YOU, WHY IS EACH READING DIFFERENT?

Each position in a layout has a different significance and there are many different layouts. Some positions refer to the past, some to various aspects of the present, and some to different possibilities in the future. Each card has a spectrum of meaning. Each position affects that meaning. So a card that refers to money could mean a background of money, an ample amount of money in the present, or money that will come in the future. The meaning of the money is also modified by the other cards in the layout. Money in the past may pertain to the family rather than to the individual client. Money in the present could relate to gains from working or to an occupation such as banking or investment counseling in which the money is not owned by the client. Money in the future might represent the desire or expectation of the client rather than a probable result of the client's actions.

The same is true for a variety of other cards. A personal characteristic associated with a particular card might mean that the client used to have that characteristic, now has it, or will have it in the future depending on the position of that card in the layout. That characteristic could also, in certain positions, be a characteristic of the activities of the client. And so forth.

IF YOU SAW SOMETHING TERRIBLE IN THE CARDS, LIKE IMMINENT DEATH, WOULD YOU TELL THE CLIENT?

Yes. I consider it my responsibility to accurately tell the client what I see in the cards. However, I would also tell the client that the future is not predetermined. What I see in the cards, I see as a possibility—never as a certainty. If I reveal to the client this "something terrible" that I see as a possibility, he or she may well know it already. If the client has a serious health problem, he may have been told the same thing by a doctor. Or the client may have a relative, friend, or associate who is severely ill or in some type of potentially dangerous situation, occupation, or activity.

I am always honest with the client because only the client can determine if the information is useful or if the news is good or bad. In the case of the possibility of death, it could be that the person whose death seems imminent may be ready for death as the alternative to prolonged suffering. I make a special effort to ensure that the client understands that Tarot readings may not accurately forecast the future, that the reading tells about a possibility that may or may not happen.

HOW OFTEN SHOULD A CLIENT GET A READING?

That depends on how rapidly things are changing in the client's life. If the client's life seems to be unfolding in an understandable or predictable way, then an annual reading might be considered useful and adequate. If the client experiences unexpected changes, the client may want to get a reading each time such change occurs. This is particularly true if readings from a known reader have proven helpful earlier.

HAS A TAROT READING EVER CHANGED YOUR LIFE?

Yes. I have had readings that made me look at the circumstances and events in my life in different and more complete ways. Particularly at crucial points of decision in my life, being shown a wider point of view opened me up to new ideas and greater possibilities that in turn led to significant changes in my life.

DO YOU READ THE CARDS FOR YOURSELF?

Yes, but the results are mixed. Since I usually know what I want to happen, I tend to interpret the cards from that bias. I find that I usually get more useful information from another reader.

17

Being the Best Reader Possible–A Review

The potential reader becomes an actual reader by a series of steps. All of these steps are important if any reader is going to become the best reader that she or he can possibly be. The first step is deciding to become a reader. No one becomes a reader by accident or chance. There has to be a conscious decision to commit time and effort toward developing the skills and abilities that a reader needs. After the decision has been made, the potential reader must obtain a Tarot deck. If the potential reader is going to be taught by someone else in a class or by individual instruction, then it is important to get a Tarot deck that the teacher accepts as appropriate. It is possible that some decks might be unacceptable to the teacher for any number of reasons. Remember that the teacher has the right to determine what teaching materials are required. If the potential reader is going to be self-taught, as many readers are, then the important factors in selecting a Tarot deck are that the reader enjoys and relates to the pictures and symbols in the deck.

Once the Tarot deck has been selected, the commitment the potential reader has made will be tested. The meanings of the cards must become part of the reader's accessible memory. Just as a person learned the alphabet, the numbers, and all the other things that became a part of the permanent accessible memory, the potential reader must spend some hours learning meanings for the cards. At first it may seem a formidable task, but anyone who is sincerely interested can do it. There are 78 cards. As the potential reader becomes more and more familiar with them, each card begins to be associated with meaning just as the face of an often-seen acquaintance is associated with a name and other related data. Use whatever methods of learning seem most productive. Eventually, after the memorization has been done over a period of time that is appropriate to the individual reader, each card becomes as well-known as a friend.

Many Tarot instructions have detailed information about rituals in relation to the cards. How the cards are stored and treated is up to the individual reader. If any such ritual is given significance by the individual reader, then that reader should follow it. If the ritual appears meaningless, the reader should feel free to ignore it. The reader's cards should be treated like any other valuable possession. Do not loan them to anyone else.

The potential reader will probably learn at least one layout while learning the meanings of the cards. Practice at least one layout until the meanings of the positions are firmly in mind. Since each position has only one meaning, this is less demanding than learning the meanings of the cards. The important thing about the layout selected is that it seems feasible to the potential reader. Any layout from any source may be used if the reader feels right about it.

Once the potential reader has some familiarity with card meanings and with one or more layouts, the next step is practice readings. These should probably first be done without a client. Have reference materials on card meanings and layout positions at hand. The reader should shuffle the deck seven times to remove any existing pattern in the deck. Cut the cards and deal them out in the selected layout.

Once the practice layout is before the reader, he or she begins looking at the cards to determine what the cards can reveal. The reader should check how many Major Arcana cards are in the layout because the Major Arcana cards are more powerful than the others. Each Major Arcana card can signify something of special importance in the reading. A high percentage of Major Arcana cards in the layout means the events and circumstances of the client's life are of great significance.

Then the reader should see how many cards of each suit of the Minor Arcana are in the reading to see which areas of life the reading will encompass. The numbered Pentacle suit cards pertain to the physical world and will reference things that can be seen and touched. The numbered Cups suit cards deal with the emotions involved. The numbered Swords cards deal with mental activity such as thinking, perceiving, reasoning, and believing. The numbered Wands cards are concerned with matters of the spirit, of aspirations, of motivational forces that guide behavior and belief. The court cards usually represent other people to be mentioned.

The reader should deliver the practice session out loud if at all possible. This will stop the reader from skipping over the meaning of any card or position and from assuming that he or she is already articulate about any portion of the reading. Taping the practice will help him or her detect any difficulties in the delivery of the material. Review the tape and visualize the layout and each card in its position. If you cannot picture the layout, the reading was incomplete. The client deserves more information.

During any practice reading, the reader may discover that the meanings of certain cards seem vague. The reader should look up the meaning in reference materials and do more memorization work. The same is true for any difficulty in remembering the significance of any position in the layout.

After a practice session, the reader should imagine what else the client might ask. Then provide answers to the imagined questions. This is an opportunity to use an expansion layout or other techniques with the cards to provide additional information.

Practice can help the reader develop his or her ability to create a coherent story representing major aspects of the client's life. The client should find the tale interesting, particularly because the client is the subject. Most clients are interested and involved in their own lives. They will make a sincere mental effort to connect what the reader says with their own life circumstances. If the client identifies the information that the reader presents with specific things in his or her life, the client is much more apt to be satisfied with the reading. This also helps the client derive the maximum benefit from it, even if the benefit is limited to entertainment.

Once the reader has the experience of enough practice, then actual readings can be performed. Usually these first readings will be for other beginning readers, relatives, friends, or acquaintances. These experiences will help the reader develop an individual style and a smooth presentation. With practice also comes confidence. The reader will begin to feel that he or she is ready and qualified to give Tarot readings in a polished manner in exchange for a fee.

Now the new reader is ready to seek clients. This can be done through advertising, word-of-mouth from satisfied clients, exposure at fairs, fund-raisers, or parties, and from being alert to other opportunities for publicity and promotion.

The new reader must develop an individual style for dealing with clients. Two major factors in style are honesty and equality. The reader has an implicit obligation to be honest with each client. Honesty means never having to remember a false frame of reference and leaving the memory free to deal with the experienced reality. Equality means treating all clients as if they are valuable and entitled to the best that can be provided in the reading. Treat them with politeness and respect as individual human beings.

One of the common difficulties that a reader will experience is the occasional client who is contemptuous of Tarot readings and Tarot readers. The reader should view this as an opportunity to show grace under pressure.

The main characteristic of skeptically hostile clients is a closed mind that they have created with a self-limiting belief system based on what they consider to be the one and only true religion, their definition of reality according to their limited understanding, or their refusal to recognize phenomena that has not been approved by themselves or other authority figures. These people do not recognize that each individual exists in a separate reality created by the individual's experience as interpreted by the individual's mind. They believe that their reality is either the only one or one that is superior to others. They falsely consider themselves arbiters of reality when all they are really doing is defending a limited belief system.

The reader should not argue with such clients and should make no attempt to change their minds. The reader should be skilled enough to avoid a useless debate. Acknowledge a willingness to accept that the client has a reality that is as useful to him or her as your reality is to you. Close the discussion without entering the client's emotionally charged world where nonproductive discussions waste everyone's time.

A minority of clients will become very emotional during a reading. The reader should be aware that this is a possibility. Usually the emotion is associated with something in the client's life that appears in the reading. The reader should accept the client's strong emotions but not attempt to stop the emotional flow or to join in it. The reader should respect the client's feelings without being swept away by them. If the client's emotions are negative and directed toward the reader, then the reader should avoid giving any emotional response that will prolong the emotional display. The reader should remember that the past exists only when you think about it. If the client's emotions are about the past then perhaps the reader can do or say something that will allow the client to think about the present. The skillful reader will avoid making any criticism that would create distance between the client and reader.

The skilled reader develops a competent, friendly manner. He or she invites the client to relax and appreciate the experience of hearing his or her life situation described in an entertaining and possibly enlightening way. The client can benefit from a different perspective of events, a wider viewpoint about life, or a clarification of the meaning or significance of his or her actions.

The benefits that the reader derives from becoming the best possible reader that he or she can be are numerous. The most obvious one is the receiving of fees. The fees may be of little importance to the reader or they may be very important. There should be a fee to compensate the reader for time and expertise as well as to convince the client that he or she is getting something of value.

Another benefit of becoming a good reader is an increase in self-esteem. The reader experiences satisfaction from successfully learning to become a reader in addition to the satisfaction that comes with giving most readings. When the reader gets new clients that were referred by other clients, the reader can take justifiable pride in his or her demonstrated abilities.

The benefit of increased popularity is important to some readers. Many people consider a reader a person worth knowing, someone they can recommend to others, and talk talk about with their friends and acquaintances. Readers are often in demand for various social events. Some people will be interested in paying for readings for visitors from out of town so that their guests will have a memorable experience and have something to talk about when they return home.

Perhaps the greatest benefit of all to the reader is an increase in intuition and knowledge. Reading Tarot cards is one of the best methods of increasing intuitive abilities. Every reading also increases the Tarot reader's knowledge of what it is to be human and of the world in ways that few other experiences can offer. Becoming the best possible Tarot reader assures you that life will be more interesting. It is one certain way to achieve personal growth and feel more fully alive.

If you are unable to find any Newcastle book at your local bookstore, please write to:

Newcastle Publishing Co., Inc.
13419 Saticoy Street
North Hollywood, CA 91605

INDIVIDUALS: To order any of the books listed in our catalog, please fill out order form, check the number of copies of each title desired, and enclose check or money order for the full amount plus $3.00 postage and handling for the first book ordered; $1.00 for each additional book. California residents please add current sales tax with each order.

VISA AND MASTERCARD ACCEPTED
$15 MINIMUM ORDER

Quantity discounts are available to groups, organizations, and companies for any Newcastle title. To telephone your orders, call (800) 932-4809 or FAX (818) 780-2007. Call (213) 873-3191 for all other inquiries.

Thank you for your interest in Newcastle.
Al Saunders, *Publisher*

OTHER BOOKS OF INTEREST
FROM NEWCASTLE PUBLISHING CO.

Haindl Tarot, Vol. 1, by Rachel Pollack, $9.95

Haindl Tarot, Vol. 2, by Rachel Pollack, $9.95

Karmic Tarot, by William Lammey, $12.95

Key of Destiny, by Homer Curtis, $9.95

Key to the Universe, by Homer Curtis, $9.95

Tarot: Apprentice, Vol. 1 (Classic), illustrated with Rider Waite deck, by Eileen Connolly, $12.95

Tarot: Apprentice, Vol. 1 (Revised), illustrated with the Connolly deck, by Eileen Connolly, $12.95

Tarot: Journeyman, Vol. 2 (Rider Waite deck), by Eileen Connolly, $12.95

Tarot for Your Self, by Mary K. Greer, $14.95

Tarot Constellations, by Mary K. Greer, $14.95

Tarot Mirrors, by Mary K. Greer, $14.95

Thursday Night Tarot, by Jason Lotterhand, $14.95

Many Tarot decks are also available from Newcastle. Please write or call for availability.